GOSPEL
MARK

EXPLORING THE LIFE OF JESUS

PROJECT ENGINEER:
Lyman Coleman

AUTHOR OF THE COMMENTARY/NOTES
Richard Peace

AUTHORS OF THE GROUP QUESTIONS
Dietrich Gruen
William Cutler
Vern Becker
Mary Naegeli
James Singleton
Denny Rydberg

PRODUCTION TEAM
John Winson
Billie Herwig
Erika Tiepel
Paul Weiland
Doug LaBudde

COVER DESIGN
Steve Eames

CARTOONIST
Robert Shull

SERENDIPITY GROUP BIBLE STUDY

Serendipity GROUP Bible Study Series
SERENDIPITY/BOX 1012/LITTLETON, CO 80160 / **TOLL FREE 800-525-9563**
In Colorado (303) 798-1313

94 95 96 / F / 10 9 8 7 6 5 4 3 2

Questions And Answers About

Starting a Bible Study Group

PURPOSE

1. *What is the purpose of a Bible study group?* Three things: (and all three are important)

   a. Nurture—to be fed by God and grow in Christ, principally through Bible study.

   b. Support—getting to know each other in a deeper way and caring for each other's needs

   c. Mission—reaching out to non-churched people who are open to studying the Bible and reaching beyond your initial number until you can split into two groups . . . and keep multiplying.

NON-CHURCHED

2. *How can people who don't go to church be interested in studying the Bible?* Pretty easy. In a recent survey, the Gallup Poll discovered that 74% of the people in America are looking for a spiritual faith.

TURNED-OFF

3. *Then, why don't they go to church?* Because they have a problem with the institutional church.

SEEKERS

4. *What are you suggesting?* That you start a Bible study group for these kinds of people:

   ● People who are turned off by the church but are looking for a spiritual faith.

   ● People who are struggling with personal problems and need a support group.

   ● People who are crippled by a bad experience with the church and want to start over in their spiritual pilgrimage.

   ● People who are down on themselves and need encouragement to see beyond their own shortcomings.

   ● People who are looking for hope in the face of seemingly insurmountable difficulties.

   ● People who flashed across your mind as you read over this list.

RECRUITING

5. *How do I get started?* Make a list of the "honest seekers you know" and keep this list on your refrigerator until you have asked everyone.

FIRST MEETING

6. *What do we do at the first meeting?* Decide on your group covenant— a "contract" that spells out your expectations and rules (see the center section, page 3).

DEVELOPING A CONTRACT

7. *How do we develop a contract?* Discuss these questions and ask someone to write down what you agree upon. (This "contract" will be used again at the close to evaluate your group).

- What is the purpose of our group?

- What are the specific goals?

- How long are we going to meet? (We recommend 6 to 12 weeks. Then, if you wish to continue, you can renew the contract.)

- Where are we going to meet?

- What is going to be the starting and ending time at the sessions?

- What about babysitting/refreshments/etc.?

LIFECYCLE

8. *How long should a Bible study group last?* This should be taken in stages. (See flow chart below)

SHORT

9. *Why only a few weeks to start with?* Because people will give priority to something if they know it's not for long. And they can always renew and keep going if they wish.

STUDY PLANS

10. *How do we go about the study of this book of the Bible?* This should be decided at the first meeting. Inside the front cover of this book are a number of options that you can choose from. You need to discuss these options and agree on your study plans.

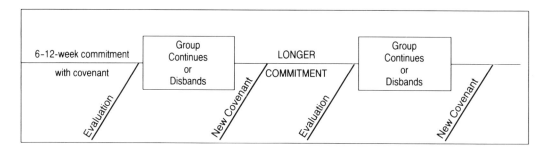

HOMEWORK	**11.** *Is there any homework?* No—unless you want to do some research about a particular concern. If you are studying one of the longer books of the Bible, where you do not have time to cover every passage, you may want to follow the "Reading" suggestions for this course of study.
BIBLE IGNORANCE	**12.** *What if we have people in the group who know nothing about the Bible?* Great. This is what this group is all about. There are NOTES on the opposite page to refer to if you have any questions about a word, historical fact or significant person in the passage.
NOTES	**13.** *Who wrote these Notes?* Richard Peace, a Professor at Gordon Conwell Seminary and a recognized Bible scholar.
SERENDIPITY	**14.** *What is Serendipity?* A small research foundation that specializes in programs for support groups in a Christian context.
DREAM	**15.** *What is your dream?* Christian support groups for hurting and struggling people inside and outside of the church—built around a study of Scripture and care for one another. For further information, we invite you to call: TOLL FREE 800-525-9563, In COLORADO 303-798-1313.

Introduction to

THE GOSPEL OF MARK

The Gospel of Mark is, according to William Barclay, "the most important book in the world." He says this, of course, because Mark is the first written account of Jesus' life and ministry. To be sure, Jesus is mentioned in documents that predate Mark. Paul's epistles contain a number of such references. But in Mark's Gospel we find for the first time an account that focuses on Jesus: who he was and what he did.

Author

The author of this Gospel is nowhere named. However, there is a strong and unbroken tradition dating from early in the second century that Mark wrote this Gospel. That a Gospel was said to be written by someone who was not an apostle is remarkable (since generally those books written by apostles were accepted as authoritative) and is strong proof in itself that he wrote it. Many hold that Mark was Peter's secretary, and that this Gospel reflects Peter's point of view. Writing around A.D. 140 (or even earlier), Bishop Papias said: "Mark, having become the interpreter of Peter, wrote down accurately all that he remembered of the things said and done by our Lord, but not however in order." And indeed, when one compares the sermons of Peter in the book of Acts with the way the Gospel unfolds, there is great similarity. Furthermore, it is evident that Mark worked with Peter in Rome and that Peter felt a warm affection for him. Peter calls him "my son Mark" (1Pe 5:13).

Who then is Mark? His full name was John Mark. He was a Jewish Christian. His mother's name was Mary and she was evidently well-to-do. The disciples used her home in Jerusalem as a meeting place in the days following Jesus' death and resurrection. After his miraculous escape from prison, the first place Peter went was to the home of Mary (Ac 12:12-17). As a young man, Mark was immersed in the life of the newly-forming church.

When Paul and Barnabus went on their first missionary journey, John Mark went with them. Barnabas was Mark's cousin (Col 4:10). Mark unaccountably left the party at Perga when they started inland to Asia. No reason is given for his departure, though it has been variously conjectured that he left because they were about to start on a notoriously dangerous road and he was afraid; or that he left because he chaffed under Paul's domination of his kinsman Barnabus. Chrysostom, the early church father, said that Mark went home because he missed his mother! In any case, this led to a sharp disagreement between Paul and Barnabas when Barnabas wanted to take Mark along on the second missionary journey. As a result, Paul and Barnabas split up. Barnabas took Mark with him to Cyprus, while Paul teamed up with Silas (Ac 15:36-41). Later on, however, Paul and Mark were reconciled so that when Paul was in prison in Rome Mark was with him. Paul also sent him on a mission to Asia Minor (Phm 24; Col 4:10). During his final imprisonment, Mark is one of the people Paul wants with him (2Ti 4:11). In his final letter to Timothy, Paul comments how helpful Mark has been to him in ministry.

Thus Mark was in an ideal position to write the first account of our Lord's life. As a young man, he may well have been an eyewitness of the final days of Jesus' life. He witnessed the founding of the first church in Jerusalem. He also worked with the two key leaders of first-century Christianity: Peter and Paul. From Peter he would have heard about Jesus (from one of the three closest to Jesus). From Paul he would have gained an appreciation for the OT roots of Christianity and sense of the significance of Jesus' life and death. Mark was evidently a very bright man (judging from the quality of his manuscript) who then took all this material, and under the guidance of the Holy Spirit, produced the first account of Jesus' life told in this new form of literature. Barclay may well be right that this is "the most important book in the world."

The Primacy of Mark

Did Mark write the first Gospel? For most of the history of the church, it was assumed that Matthew's Gospel was written first (hence the order of the four Gospels in our Bibles). However, based on the research of scholars in the earlier part of the century, it now seems more likely that Mark wrote first and that Luke and Matthew copied large chunks of his work. It is clear that there is a literary connection between the three synoptic Gospels (Matthew, Mark, and Luke) since they share so much common material. For example, even the parenthesis in the story of the healing of the paralytic—"He said to the paralytic"—is in the identical place in all three accounts (see Mt 9:6, Mk 2:10, and Lk 5:24). All but 24 verses of Mark appear in the other two synoptics. To put this another way: there are 105 sections in Mark, and all but 4 occur in Matthew or Luke. In fact, Matthew uses nearly 90% of the sections in Mark (93 of the 105) including not just the same stories, but 51% of Mark's very words.

The problem comes in explaining the nature of this connection. This is a complex question, but the best guess is that Matthew and Luke used what Mark wrote, polished up the language, and then added new material on the teaching of Jesus.

Date and Audience

When it comes to ancient manuscripts, it is difficult to pinpoint exactly when they were written. However, it is almost certain that Mark wrote his Gospel sometime between A.D. 50 and 70. It is clear from the text that he wrote to Greek-speaking readers who were not familiar with Jewish customs (see 7:3-4; 12:18; and 14:12 for examples of how Mark explains Jewish customs). Beyond this, we do not know for sure who his audience is or why he wrote, since he does not tell us in his Gospel.

One good guess is that Mark was written to Christians living in Rome following the disastrous fire in that city in A.D. 64. This is what William Lane contends in his excellent commentary on Mark. And it does seem as if Mark was in Rome with Peter at the time of the crisis under Nero (see 1Pe 5:13).

Lane points out that for a long time, Christians were fairly anonymous in the Roman Empire. When and if they were noticed, it was assumed that they were just another exotic religious sect, of which there were many in the first century. They were often thought to be a splinter group within Judaism. But all this changed after Nero burned down Rome. Despite the generous aid he gave to the victims of the fire and the widespread urban renewal that followed the fire (in which he widened the roads, put in parks and rebuilt the city with fireproof construction materials), Nero continued to be blamed for the fire. Suetonius, the Roman historian, wrote that Nero "set fire to the city so openly that several former consuls did not venture to lay hands on his chamberlains although they caught them on their estates with tow and firebands."

To quell this criticism, Nero needed a scapegoat and the Christians were chosen for this dubious honor. As Lane says, Nero introduced the Church to martyrdom. Tacitus wrote about the events in that day:

> Neither human resources, nor imperial munificence, nor appeasement of the gods, eliminated sinister suspicions that the fire had been instigated. To suppress this rumor, Nero fabricated scapegoats—and punished with every refinement the notoriously depraved Christians (as they were popularly called)....First, Nero had self-acknowledged Christians arrested. Then, on their information, large numbers of others were condemned—not so much for incendiarism as for their anti-social tendencies. Their deaths were made farcical. Dressed in wild animals' skins, they were torn to pieces by dogs, or crucified, or made into torches to be ignited after dark as substitutes for daylight. Nero provided his Gardens for the spectacle....Despite their guilt as Christians, and the ruthless punishment it deserved, the victims were pitied. For it was felt that they were being sacrificed to one man's brutality rather than to the national interest.

If this was indeed the motivation for the writing of this Gospel, then what Mark has done is to put together the story of our Lord so as to guide and comfort the dying Christians. And indeed one finds in this Gospel many parallels between what the Christians in Rome were going through and what happened in the life of our Lord. He too suffered. He too had wilderness experiences. He too was misunderstood, betrayed, misused by officialdom, and finally, killed. But—and this is the hope that Mark brings—his death was not in vain. In fact, his death was what his life was all about. It was by his death that his ministry was successfully completed. That his death had a purpose in God's scheme of things must have brought great comfort to the martyrs in Rome.

Themes

And certainly the death of Jesus is one of the central themes in this Gospel. In fact, Mark's Gospel has been called "a passion-narrative with an extended introduction." Of the 16 chapters, over one-third focus on the last week of Jesus' life and the events surrounding the crucifixion. Furthermore, right from the beginning of the Gospel, the coming death of Jesus is present like a bass note throbbing beneath the action.

In fact, as the Gospel unfolds it becomes evident that who Jesus is will not become clear until his crucifixion. This is one reason why Jesus keeps silencing the demons who know him. People would misunderstand unless they knew he came to die. Even the Twelve do not understand fully who Jesus is prior to his death.

This leads to a second theme within this Gospel: Jesus as the teacher of the Twelve. We watch as the Lord calls the Twelve to join his band and then gradually reveals to them who he is. At first they don't understand. They see him as just a better-than-average rabbi: a teacher with unusual gifts to teach, heal, and cast out demons. Then they realize that his powers extend far beyond those of a rabbi. He has power over the elements, over evil, over disease, and even over death itself. It dawns on them that he is the Messiah. But even then they do not understand what kind of Messiah he is. They are thinking of the Messiah as conquering hero who will oust Rome and set up his kingdom in Jerusalem. Jesus must teach them that instead he has come to suffer and die. They never understand this—at least, not until he does indeed die and rise again. So, in Mark we see Jesus as the skilled teacher who must overcome the cultural bias and personal ambitions of the Twelve in order that they will come to see him for who he truly is.

A third theme in the book emerges from these two. Mark is all about what it means to be a disciple of Jesus. It is not what the Twelve expected—all glory and triumph. To follow the one who came as a suffering servant who gave himself for others is to take up one's cross as the Lord did. There is a profound view of the Christian life in this Gospel.

Genre and Focus

Mark created a new style of literature. This is the first example of a "Gospel"; i.e., a historical narrative of the life of Jesus with theological intention. A Gospel is not a biography, in that it omits much of what we have come to expect in that type of writing. There is no mention in Mark of the childhood of Jesus, of what he looked like, of who his friends were, of what events shaped his early imagination, etc. Instead, Mark plunges straightway into the adult life of Jesus. In fact, he only deals with the last three years of his life. Even within that narrow focus, Mark is highly selective. He focuses primarily on one event: the death of Jesus. The story of Jesus' final week occupies over one-third of the story.

A Gospel is an account of the life of Jesus "with theological intent." By this is meant that each Gospel writer has his own vantage point. Matthew wrote to a Jewish audience and told the story of King Jesus, the son of David, who came as the long expected Messiah. Luke wrote about the Son of Man who came to seek and save the needy and the outcasts. John wrote about

Jesus, the divine Son of God. Mark, however, focuses on Jesus the suffering servant who died for the sake of others. Mark wrote to Gentile Christians who themselves were suffering and dying and to whom it would be a great encouragement to remember that their Lord, in whose name they are dying, walked the same path as they.

Style

Mark's style of writing is distinctive. He uses short, punchy sentences often linked together by the word "and." His verbs are active and his pace is rapid. Yet, despite the way he hurries through the material, his account is rich in vivid eyewitness detail. For example, when Mark tells us about the blessing of the children, he alone points out that Jesus first took the children into his arms (Mk 10:13-16).

An interesting thing that Mark does is to sandwich a story in between the beginning and the end of another story. For example, the first time he does this is in 3:20-35. He begins by talking about the concerns the Jesus' family had and their decision "take charge of him." In between this decision and their arrival at his place of ministry, Mark relates the story of how the teachers of the law concluded that Jesus was possessed by Beelzebub. The section ends with Jesus' family outside the house asking for him. Mark interposes two stories when they interconnect and interpret each other.

Central to the Gospel as a literary genre is what Lightfoot calls the "little stories" that make up the account. Rather than a running narrative, a Gospel is a series of stories about Jesus pieced together by each author. Sometimes the same stories are used in different ways in different Gospels. These "little stories" (or pericopes) are, of course, what the Christian community memorized and re-told to one other. Out of the great pool of stories about Jesus, Mark selects certain ones and puts them in a particular order that will communicate what he wants to say about Jesus.

Outline

In Mark's Gospel there is a very careful and deliberate ordering of the stories. The result is a skillfully crafted outline. In fact, he has told the story of Jesus in a highly skilled and remarkably sophisticated way. This cannot have been easy given the material he had to use. Mark could not sit down and start from scratch to tell Jesus' story. Rather, he had to use the stories everyone knew in the way they knew them. He could not alter them. He was merely the chronicler of the tradition, not the creator of it. The church would not have used his work if it contained spurious tales or if he had mistold stories. No, Mark's creativity under the guidance of the Holy Spirit came at the level of choosing which stories to set next to each other. As you read through the Gospel, be alert to the significance of the sequence of stories as they unfold.

Mark does not put his stories in chronological order as we might expect, given the way history is written today (though overall there is a rough chronology to the story). Instead, he groups his stories thematically. Mark uses several organizing principles simultaneously. For one thing, it is clear that he has structured his story *geographically*. Jesus' ministry begins up north in Galilee and then he moves down to Jerusalem, where he is finally killed. Mark also structures the story in terms of *Jesus' unfolding ministry*: preparation, proclamation, and completion. There is also an unfolding vision of *who Jesus is*. In broad terms, the first half of the book focuses on the discovery of Jesus as the Messiah, and the second half on the discovery of Jesus as the Son of God. In terms of the *disciples' growing awareness*, they move from experiencing Jesus as an exceptional rabbi, to seeing him as a man of power, and then as the healer of hardened hearts. After Cesarea Philippi and their realization that he is the Messiah, they next know him as a teacher. In Jerusalem during the final week of his life, they come to realize that he is the Son of God.

UNIT 1   John the Baptist/The Baptism and Temptation of Jesus

Mark 1:1-13

John the Baptist Prepares the Way

1 The beginning of the gospel about Jesus Christ, the Son of God. [a]

[2]It is written in Isaiah the prophet:

"I will send my messenger ahead of you,
    who will prepare your way" [b]—
[3]"a voice of one calling in the desert,
'Prepare the way for the Lord,
    make straight paths for him.' " [c]

[4]And so John came, baptizing in the desert region and preaching a baptism of repentance for the forgiveness of sins. [5]The whole Judean countryside and all the people of Jerusalem went out to him. Confessing their sins, they were baptized by him in the Jordan River. [6]John wore clothing made of camel's hair, with a leather belt around his waist, and he ate locusts and wild honey. [7]And this was his message: "After me will come one more powerful than I, the thongs of whose sandals I am not worthy to stoop down and untie. [8]I baptize you with [d] water, but he will baptize you with the Holy Spirit."

The Baptism and Temptation of Jesus

[9]At that time Jesus came from Nazareth in Galilee and was baptized by John in the Jordan. [10]As Jesus was coming up out of the water, he saw heaven being torn open and the Spirit descending on him like a dove. [11]And a voice came from heaven: "You are my Son, whom I love; with you I am well pleased."

[12]At once the Spirit sent him out into the desert, [13]and he was in the desert forty days, being tempted by Satan. He was with the wild animals, and angels attended him.

Questions

OPEN: 1. Whose character sketch fits you best: Charlie Brown? Snoopy? Lucy? Schroeder? Peppermint Patty? Sally? Linus? Pig Pen? Fill in the sketch for the group. **2.** As a child, what dream of grandeur did you imagine about yourself as an adult?

DIG: Read the Introduction and leaf through Mark. Note captions and other clues to the book's meaning. **1.** What are some things to look for in this book? What are your first impressions? The principle characters? Key events? **2.** What do the contexts of the quotes (see notes) teach about the "coming one"? **3.** Why is John's ministry so popular (vv.4-5)? **4.** What does John's clothing and diet say about him (v.6; see 2Ki 1:8; Mal 4:5)? **5.** Given John's message (vv.7-8), what type of person is the crowd anticipating (see Isa 32:15-20)? How do these expectations account for the crowd's reception of John, despite his hard message? **6.** What do you think the dove and voice (vv.10-11) meant to Jesus as he came out of the water? As he entered the desert? During his temptations? How would all this prepare him?

REFLECT: 1. What illustration from your life describes what it means to repent? **2.** What was the beginning point in the *Gospel According to You*? Who was your John the Baptist? **3.** What "spiritual wilderness" has God sent you into? What has that done for your sense of his love and mission?

[a]1 Some manuscripts do not have *the Son of God.*   [b]2 Mal. 3:1   [c]3 Isaiah 40:3
[d]8 Or *in*

Notes

1:1-13 In this short prologue, Mark tells of Jesus' preparation for ministry. The brevity of this prologue stands in sharp contrast to Matthew and Luke, each of whom devotes over 4 chapters to the period in Jesus' life prior to the start of his ministry.

1:2-3 The Jews expected that an Elijah-like figure would precede the Messiah and announce his coming (see Mal 3:1,4:5; Mk 9:4). In typical rabbinical fashion, Mark has combined several OT texts—Mal 3:1 (v.2) and Isa 40:3 (v.3)—by which he shows that John's coming was foretold, that this "messenger" would pave the way for the Lord, and thus that Jesus was, indeed, the long promised Messiah.

1:4 *And so John came*. The promised messenger turns out to be John the Baptist. ***baptizing***. When Gentiles converted to Judaism they were required to bathe in a river as part of the ceremony. This signified that—in a symbolic way—their sins had been washed away. It was highly unusual, however, for *Jews* to submit to such a rite, and the fact that they did signals, perhaps, the desperation they felt at that point in history. ***the desert region***. This was the term used for a particular area in Israel located in the lower Jordan Valley between central Judea and the Dead Sea. This region was some 10 to 15 miles wide and extended for nearly 60 miles. It was a desolate and blistering hot place, consisting of jagged limestone precipices and sparse vegetation. It was not a nice place to live!

1:5 *The whole Judean countryside*. Mark uses a hyperbole (lit. "*all* the Judean country") to show John's enormous popularity. Israel had been without a prophet for more than 300 years, and John certainly looked and talked like a prophet. ***All the people of Jerusalem***. It was a difficult 20 mile trip from Jerusalem to where John was baptizing, and yet the crowds came.

1:6 This description is similar to that of OT prophets (e.g., 2Ki 1:8). ***locusts and wild honey***. The locusts he ate could be either an insect (Lev 11:22-23) or a kind of bean from the locust tree. Honey could refer either to what bees produce or to the sap of a certain tree. In either case, this was the food eaten by the poorest of people.

1:9 *At that time Jesus came*. In the midst of this supercharged atmosphere—one foretold by OT prophets (vv.2-3), prepared by a NT prophet (vv.4,6-7), and witnessed by the expectant crowds (v.5)—Jesus starts his ministry. The subsequent drama of his baptism and temptation (vv.9-13) bring in to this already impressive scene a supernatural host—God the Father, God the Holy Spirit and, of course, God the Son (v.11), as well as angels and Satan himself (v.13). ***baptized***. By allowing himself to be baptized, Jesus identified with the people of Israel and with their sin (though he himself was without sin— 1Pe 2:22), prefiguring his death for sin a few years hence.

1:11 *a voice*. These words from God are directed to Jesus, not to the crowds. They are an unqualified affirmation of him as he is about to launch his ministry. In the days ahead it will be Jesus' task to make known to Israel who he is.

1:12 *the spirit sent him*. The same Spirit who had come to Jesus in such affirming power now sends him forth to this time of testing.

1:13 *tempted*. This was a trial of strength between the Son of God and Satan, not a moral test to see if Jesus would give into sin. ***wild animals***. For the Christians to whom this letter was written (who were facing wild beasts in the Roman Coliseum), it must have been comforting to know that Jesus had also faced such beasts and was sustained by angels.

UNIT 2 The Calling of the First Disciples/ Jesus Drives Out an Evil Spirit/ Jesus Heals Many/A Man With Leprosy

Mark 1:14-45

The Calling of the First Disciples

¹⁴After John was put in prison, Jesus went into Galilee, proclaiming the good news of God. ¹⁵"The time has come," he said. "The kingdom of God is near. Repent and believe the good news!"

¹⁶As Jesus walked beside the Sea of Galilee, he saw Simon and his brother Andrew casting a net into the lake, for they were fishermen. ¹⁷"Come, follow me," Jesus said, "and I will make you fishers of men." ¹⁸At once they left their nets and followed him.

¹⁹When he had gone a little farther, he saw James son of Zebedee and his brother John in a boat, preparing their nets. ²⁰Without delay he called them, and they left their father Zebedee in the boat with the hired men and followed him.

Jesus Drives Out an Evil Spirit

²¹They went to Capernaum, and when the Sabbath came, Jesus went into the synagogue and began to teach. ²²The people were amazed at his teaching, because he taught them as one who had authority, not as the teachers of the law. ²³Just then a man in their synagogue who was possessed by an evil' spirit cried out, ²⁴"What do you want with us, Jesus of Nazareth? Have you come to destroy us? I know who you are—the Holy One of God!"

²⁵"Be quiet!" said Jesus sternly. "Come out of him!" ²⁶The evil spirit shook the man violently and came out of him with a shriek.

²⁷The people were all so amazed that they asked each other, "What is this? A new teaching—and with authority! He even gives orders to evil spirits and they obey him." ²⁸News about him spread quickly over the whole region of Galilee.

Jesus Heals Many

²⁹As soon as they left the synagogue, they went with James and John to the home of Simon and Andrew. ³⁰Simon's mother-in-law was in bed with a fever, and they told Jesus about her. ³¹So he went to her, took her hand and helped her up. The fever left her and she began to wait on them.

³²That evening after sunset the people brought to Jesus all the sick and demon-possessed. ³³The whole town gathered at the door, ³⁴and Jesus healed many who had various diseases. He also drove out many demons, but he would not let the demons speak because they knew who he was.

Questions

OPEN: 1. Who is the best fisherman in your extended family? 2. Where did you go the first time you really "left home"?

DIG: 1. Why would Jesus begin his public ministry in Galilee (see notes)? 2. What is the "good news" according to Jesus? How does this compare to the message of John the Baptist? 3. What would the disciples understand at this point by "kingdom of God"? By "fishers of men"? 4. In verses 21-25, why do you suppose Jesus started his public ministry in a synagogue? What two things about Jesus amazed the people? Why? 5. What does it mean to teach "with authority"? What was the nature and source of Jesus' authority? Likewise, of this "evil spirit"? 6. How does Jesus' healing (vv.30-31) compare with his exorcism (v.25)? What new realm of authority is seen here? 7. How do you picture the scene in verses 32-34? Why does he silence the demons? 8. After a day like this (vv.29-34), what pressures would Jesus feel as a new day dawns? What might he pray about? How might this relate to his decision (v.38)? 9. As Simon, how do you feel about that decision? 10. How does this healing of the leper relate to the rest of this chapter (see notes)? 11. Why is the leper unsure of Jesus' desire to help (see Lev 13)? What is significant about Jesus' touching the leper prior to healing him? 12. Why did he not keep silent? What happened as a result?

[Scripture and questions continued on page 14]

'23 Greek *unclean*; also in verses 26 and 27

12

Notes

1:14-45 Mark begins his account of Jesus' ministry with a series of incidents, each of which points out how quickly and how enthusiastically the people responded to Jesus.

1:14-15 His preparation complete, Jesus begins his ministry. These are transition verses in which Mark defines the nature of Jesus' ministry and summarizes his message.

1:14 *After John was put in prison*. There is a gap of perhaps a year between the incidents recorded in 1:9-13 and those recorded here. ***Galilee***. This was the northern province of Palestine. It was small, some 25 by 35 miles in size with a population (in the time of Jesus) of approximately 350,000 (100,000 of whom were Jews). Galilee was a rich farming and fishing region. Its Jewish population was considered rebellious in spirit, and lax when it came to religious matters. Those living in Jerusalem considered Galilee a cultural backwater populated by unsophisticated, uneducated country folk who spoke with an accent.

1:15 *The time has come*. That event—long expected and desired—had now come to pass in Israel. It was the fullness of time and the Messiah had entered history. ***kingdom of God***. The Jews regarded themselves as God's special people. He alone was their King. Yet they were under the domination of Rome. Caesar functioned as their king. Still, they were confident that one day the Messiah would rescue them. They fantasized that he would be a bloody warrior-king with invincible power who would lead Israel to a military victory and then establish Jerusalem as the capital of the world. It will take Jesus' whole ministry to show that he is not this sort of Messiah. In the end, it took his death and resurrection before even his disciples saw that he had quite a different sort of kingdom in mind.

1:17 Jesus calls these men in terms they could understand. In asking them to "follow" him, he was inviting them to join his band of disciples. Simon and Andrew would have been familiar with rabbis who had small groups of followers. In telling them he would make them "fishers of men," he defined their task using a metaphor they understood: they would be seeking converts to his teaching.

1:18 *At once they left*. According to 1:14 Jesus had been preaching in Galilee. These fishermen probably had the chance to hear his message prior to their call. Still, what they did was an act of great faith and courage. In the first century you lived where you were born, you stayed in your family cluster, and you took up your father's occupation.

1:20 *the hired men*. James and John came from a middle-class family. Their father Zebedee had men working for him and a boat with which to trawl the lake for fish. (See Lk 5:3,10, where it appears that Simon also had a boat.)

1:21-28 With his four newly-chosen disciples present, Jesus' first public act of ministry recorded by Mark occurs in a synagogue. Here, with God's chosen people assembled, Jesus makes his presence known by the quality of his teaching and by his extraordinary power over the demonic.

1:21 *Capernaum*. A town on the north end of the Sea of Galilee, three miles west of the River Jordan. It was a center of the fishing industry and the site of a custom's post. ***synagogue***. In first-century Israel, the temple in Jerusalem was the sole site for sacrifices and was attended by numerous priests and other officials. In contrast, there were synagogues in each population center which people attended each week for worship and instruction. Synagogues were run by lay committees with no professional clergy. Anyone could speak as long as he had permission from the leaders.

1:23 *an evil spirit*. Malignant, supernatural beings, able to harm and even possess people. These were Satan's legions. In overcoming this evil spirit, Jesus demonstrated his power over Satan. This is the opening encounter in what would be a ongoing battle.

1:24 *What do you want with us*. At first the evil spirit is defiant and resistant. ***I know who you are***. By identifying Jesus, first using his human name and then his divine title, the demon hoped to gain mastery over Jesus. It was believed that knowledge of a person's true identity (or secret name) gave one power over that person. It does not work with Jesus however! ***the Holy One of God***. The evil spirit recognizes Jesus for who he is—the divine Son of God. In contrast, it will be quite some time before anyone, even the disciples, understands this.

[Notes continued on page 15]   13

Mark 1:14-45, continued

Questions

Jesus Prays in a Solitary Place

[35]Very early in the morning, while it was still dark, Jesus got up, left the house and went off to a solitary place, where he prayed. [36]Simon and his companions went to look for him, [37]and when they found him, they exclaimed: "Everyone is looking for you!"

[38]Jesus replied, "Let us go somewhere else—to the nearby villages—so I can preach there also. That is why I have come." [39]So he traveled throughout Galilee, preaching in their synagogues and driving out demons.

A Man With Leprosy

[40]A man with leprosy[f] came to him and begged him on his knees, "If you are willing, you can make me clean."

[41]Filled with compassion, Jesus reached out his hand and touched the man. "I am willing," he said. "Be clean!" [42]Immediately the leprosy left him and he was cured.

[43]Jesus sent him away at once with a strong warning: [44]"See that you don't tell this to anyone. But go, show yourself to the priest and offer the sacrifices that Moses commanded for your cleansing, as a testimony to them." [45]Instead he went out and began to talk freely, spreading the news. As a result, Jesus could no longer enter a town openly but stayed outside in lonely places. Yet the people still came to him from everywhere.

REFLECT: 1. If the disciples show what it means to "repent and believe," where are you: (a) Still fishing? (b) Keeping the old business going and spending nights and weekends with Jesus? (c) Swimming to shore? Explain. **2.** What have you left to follow him? **3.** What about this kingdom of God "amazes" you? **4.** On a scale of one to ten, how much authority does Jesus have in your life? What would he have to "cast out" to rate a ten?

---

[f]40 The Greek word was used for various diseases affecting the skin—not necessarily leprosy.

Notes, continued

1:27 Mark notes the two things about Jesus that caught the attention of the people: the quality of his teaching and the power of his actions. **amazed**. A word used repeatedly in Mark to describe the response of the people to Jesus: here to his word of power, and previously (in v.22) to his word of instruction. Their amazement, however, contains not only joy but some alarm (even fear). Who is this man who possesses such unsuspected power?

1:28 News about him spread. People witnessed amazing power and heard extraordinary teaching, so it is not at all surprising that they told everyone they met what happened in the synagogue.

1:31 took her hand. A detail that only an eyewitness such as Peter would know about. **The fever left her**. This was a real, immediate cure. She suffered none of the weakness that normally follows when a fever breaks. **wait on them**. In a Jewish home, unless a family was wealthy enough to have servants, the women would prepare and serve the meal. Understandably, Peter's mother-in-law would have been anxious to have everything in order, since her son-in-law was bringing home such an important guest.

1:32 after sunset. Since healing was forbidden on the Sabbath, they came only after the sun set, signalling the end of the Sabbath.

1:34 drove out many demons. First-century exorcists used elaborate incantations, special spells and magic apparatus to cast out demons, in contrast to Jesus, whose word alone sufficed. **would not let the demons speak**. Before Jesus could allow himself to be identified, he had to make sure that people knew what kind of Messiah he was. He was not the bloody, militaristic Messiah imagined in the apocalyptic literature of the day. He had come instead to serve, suffer, and ultimately, to die.

1:35 he prayed. In the midst of great success, Jesus is quick to acknowledge his dependence on God as the source of his power.

1:38 With this verse Mark ends his account of an incredibly busy day in the life of Jesus. **so I can preach there also**. Jesus is determined to carry on his central mission, which is proclaiming ("preach") the kingdom of God (see vv.14-15). **let us go**. Thus Jesus begins his preaching tour of Galilee. His was to be an itinerant ministry.

1:40-45 Mark ends the first chapter with an account of a powerful healing. Jesus once again does battle with the power of evil (since disease is a form of possession by Satan). Leprosy is a particularly apt illustration of the nature of Satan's work. It brings with it progressive disintegration—both physical and psychological.

1:40 leprosy. No disease was dreaded more than leprosy, since it brought not only physical disfigurement but social banishment. **came to him**. What the leper did was forbidden by law.

1:41 Filled with compassion. Human suffering evoked a deep, affective response from Jesus. He was not afraid of strong emotions. **touched**. Actually touching a leper was unimaginable to most first-century people. Not only did one risk contracting the disease, but such contact made the well person ritually impure and thus unable to participate in the religious life of the community. The effect of Jesus' touch on this leper must have been overwhelming.

1:44 offer the sacrifices. In Leviticus 14:1-32 the ritual is outlined whereby a leper is declared "clean." Such certification was vital to a leper: it was that person's way back into normal contact with human society.

1:45 talk freely. Jesus' plea was to no avail. The leper's joy could not be contained. He told everyone how he came to be healed. **lonely places**. Mark began this cycle of stories with Jesus emerging from the wilderness in order to start his ministry. This section ends with him back in a place of isolation, driven there by the disobedience of the leper (understandable though it may be) and thus hindered in his Galilean ministry. **the people still came to him**. This is the point which Mark wants to make in this opening description of Jesus' ministry: Jesus is immensely popular with the common people. In his next section (2:1-3:6), Mark will show that, in contrast, he was not at all popular with the religious leaders.

UNIT 3 Jesus Heals a Paralytic/ The Calling of Levi

Mark 2:1-17

Jesus Heals a Paralytic

2 A few days later, when Jesus again entered Capernaum, the people heard that he had come home. ²So many gathered that there was no room left, not even outside the door, and he preached the word to them. ³Some men came, bringing to him a paralytic, carried by four of them. ⁴Since they could not get him to Jesus because of the crowd, they made an opening in the roof above Jesus and, after digging through it, lowered the mat the paralyzed man was lying on. ⁵When Jesus saw their faith, he said to the paralytic, "Son, your sins are forgiven."

⁶Now some teachers of the law were sitting there, thinking to themselves, ⁷"Why does this fellow talk like that? He's blaspheming! Who can forgive sins but God alone?"

⁸Immediately Jesus knew in his spirit that this was what they were thinking in their hearts, and he said to them, "Why are you thinking these things? ⁹Which is easier: to say to the paralytic, 'Your sins are forgiven,' or to say, 'Get up, take your mat and walk'? ¹⁰But that you may know that the Son of Man has authority on earth to forgive sins . . . ." He said to the paralytic, ¹¹"I tell you, get up, take your mat and go home." ¹²He got up, took his mat and walked out in full view of them all. This amazed everyone and they praised God, saying, "We have never seen anything like this!"

The Calling of Levi

¹³Once again Jesus went out beside the lake. A large crowd came to him, and he began to teach them. ¹⁴As he walked along, he saw Levi son of Alphaeus sitting at the tax collector's booth. "Follow me," Jesus told him, and Levi got up and followed him.

¹⁵While Jesus was having dinner at Levi's house, many tax collectors and "sinners" were eating with him and his disciples, for there were many who followed him. ¹⁶When the teachers of the law who were Pharisees saw him eating with the "sinners" and tax collectors, they asked his disciples: "Why does he eat with tax collectors and 'sinners'?"

¹⁷On hearing this, Jesus said to them, "It is not the healthy who need a doctor, but the sick. I have not come to call the righteous, but sinners."

Questions

OPEN: If in trouble in the middle of the night, which four friends would you call, and why?

DIG: 1. What would you be seeing and feeling if you were in this crowd (vv.1-4)? What was going on in the mind of the owner of the house? The paralytic? The teachers of the law? **2.** Why are the teachers so upset? In their minds, how are sin and the authority of God linked (see Jn 9:1-3)? **3.** Why didn't Jesus simply heal the man like everyone expected? What new insight about the kingdom and himself is he revealing? **4.** On the calling of Levi (vv.13-17), consider that the fishermen disciples (1:16-19) may have paid inflated taxes to Levi for years. How would they feel when Jesus called him? Why did he do so? What did it cost him? **5.** Who are the "sinners"? The "sick"? The "righteous"? Who enters God's kingdom, and why?

REFLECT: 1. How "sick" were you before you saw your need for a spiritual doctor? **2.** What from this story can you practice in your outreach (e.g., who will you invite for dinner next week)?

Notes

2:1 *A few days later*. Each of the five incidents in 2:1–3:6 is introduced by this sort of indefinite time measure (2:13,18,23; 3:1), indicating that these incidents probably did not happen in sequence, one right after the other. *home*. Jesus' base for his travels in Galilee, quite possibly Peter and Andrew's house (1:29,32–33).

2:4 *an opening in the roof*. The roof of a typical Palestinian house was flat (it was often used for sleeping) and was reached by an outside ladder or stairway. It was constructed of earth and brushwood that was packed between wooden beams set about 3 feet apart. The roof was easily breached (and easily repaired). A rather large opening would have been required to lower a man on a mat. While this was going on, with the noise and falling dirt, all attention inside would have been diverted from Jesus' sermon to the ever-growing hole. *mat*. The bed of a poor person.

2:5 *your sins are forgiven*. This was not what the crowd expected Jesus to say. They thought he would say, "You are healed." Jesus says this so as to declare to the religious leaders who he is.

2:6 *teachers of the law*. Lit. "Scribes," religious lawyers who interpreted Jewish law. Originally, it was their job to make copies of the OT. Because of their familiarity with Scripture, people consulted them about points of law and hence their role evolved into that of teacher of the law.

2:7 *this fellow*. Used as a term of contempt. *blaspheming*. Blasphemy is "contempt for God," and under Jewish law its penalty is death (see Lev 24:16). The teachers of the law believed that illness was the direct result of sin (e.g., Jn 9:2), so that the sick could not recover until their sin had been forgiven by God. They also knew that God alone could offer forgiveness. Hence they are distressed that Jesus has said to the paralytic "your sins are forgiven." This was to claim in quite explicit terms that he was divine and this was, in their eyes, the vilest blasphemy.

2:9 *which is easier*. Jesus responds to their question (v.7) in typical rabbinic fashion: he asks them a question. The answer to his question is obvious. It is far easier to *say*, "Your sins are forgiven" than it is to *heal* the man right then and there. There is no way to verify whether sins have

been forgiven, but it is obvious whether a lame man walks or not.

2:10 *but that you may know*. If Jesus is able to heal the paralytic, in terms of their own theology (which linked forgiveness and healing), the Scribes would have to admit that he had, indeed, forgiven the man's sins. For the Scribes, in other words, the visible healing verified the invisible forgiveness. If they were consistent, the teachers of the law would now have to admit that Jesus was God (or at least a representative of God), because it is they who said, "Who can forgive sins but God alone?" (v.7).

2:14 *Levi*. Elsewhere he is identified as Matthew (Mt 9:9), the disciple who eventually wrote one of the Gospels. People would have considered Matthew a disastrous selection as a disciple. In his role as tax collector, he was hated by both the religious establishment and the common people.

2:15 *having dinner*. To share a meal with another was a significant event, implying acceptance of that person. In this way, Jesus extends his forgiveness (see 2:10) to those who were outside orthodox religious life. *tax collectors*. They were hated by the Jews for collecting taxes on behalf of pagan Rome and for growing rich by collecting more than was actually required (only they knew the tax rate) and keeping the extra. Tax collectors were considered as vile as robbers or murderers. *"sinners."* A slang phrase for those who failed to observe religious practices. These were generally the common people who had to work for a living and thus did not have enough time to keep all the ritual law (e.g., they did not wash their hands in a special, complicated way before a meal).

2:16 *Why does he eat...* This is the second question asked of Jesus. They could not understand how a truly religious person could eat with rabble who might serve food not prepared according to ritual, on dishes that were ritually (though not literally) unclean.

2:17 Jesus responds by way of a metaphor laced with irony. At first glance, the Pharisees would perhaps have considered this a reasonable explanation of his behavior: he came to heal those who were sick—which to them meant the "sinners" with whom he ate. In later reflection they might come to wonder if perhaps Jesus considered them the sick ones.

UNIT 4　Jesus Questioned About Fasting/ Lord of the Sabbath

Mark 2:18-3:6

Jesus Questioned About Fasting

[18]Now John's disciples and the Pharisees were fasting. Some people came and asked Jesus, "How is it that John's disciples and the disciples of the Pharisees are fasting, but yours are not?" [19]Jesus answered, "How can the guests of the bridegroom fast while he is with them? They cannot, so long as they have him with them. [20]But the time will come when the bridegroom will be taken from them, and on that day they will fast.

[21]"No one sews a patch of unshrunk cloth on an old garment. If he does, the new piece will pull away from the old, making the tear worse. [22]And no one pours new wine into old wineskins. If he does, the wine will burst the skins, and both the wine and the wineskins will be ruined. No, he pours new wine into new wineskins."

Lord of the Sabbath

[23]One Sabbath Jesus was going through the grainfields, and as his disciples walked along, they began to pick some heads of grain. [24]The Pharisees said to him, "Look, why are they doing what is unlawful on the Sabbath?"

[25]He answered, "Have you never read what David did when he and his companions were hungry and in need? [26]In the days of Abiathar the high priest, he entered the house of God and ate the consecrated bread, which is lawful only for priests to eat. And he also gave some to his companions."

[27]Then he said to them, "The Sabbath was made for man, not man for the Sabbath. [28]So the Son of Man is Lord even of the Sabbath."

3 Another time he went into the synagogue, and a man with a shriveled hand was there. [2]Some of them were looking for a reason to accuse Jesus, so they watched him closely to see if he would heal him on the Sabbath. [3]Jesus said to the man with the shriveled hand, "Stand up in front of everyone."

[4]Then Jesus asked them, "Which is lawful on the Sabbath: to do good or to do evil, to save life or to kill?" But they remained silent.

[5]He looked around at them in anger and, deeply distressed at their stubborn hearts, said to the man, "Stretch out your hand." He stretched it out, and his hand was completely restored. [6]Then the Pharisees went out and began to plot with the Herodians how they might kill Jesus.

Questions

OPEN: Do you "fix and mend" or "toss and replace"? Why?

DIG: 1. Why did John's disciples and the Pharisees fast? Jesus' disciples didn't fast—what does that imply? **2.** How do the three mini-parables (vv.19-22) answer the question? What is the new wine? The old wineskins? **3.** In verses 23-27, what is the beef about Jesus? **4.** How does David's story apply to Jesus' situation (see 1Sa 21:1-6)? **5.** What causes the tension in the synagogue (vv. 3:1-6)? What concerns are shared by the leaders? By Jesus? By the man with the shriveled hand? **6.** What prompts Jesus' anger? **7.** Review the five conflicts recorded in 2:1-3:6. How does the opposition to Jesus grow? Why? What is the irony in 3:4-6?

REFLECT: 1. How has the "wine" of Jesus burst some of your "old wineskins"? Where is the wine bursting out right now? **2.** How have you seen religious rules or institutions hurt people? What causes that? **3.** Based on the precedent set by Jesus here and by David earlier, when would it be right for you to get angry at arbitrary rules and put human need above law (e.g., would you "steal" food to feed your starving family)? **4.** What is the "shriveled hand" that Jesus is healing in your life now?

Notes

2:18 *the Pharisees*. Members of a small (about 6,000 members at the time of Herod) but powerful religious sect whose prime concern was knowing and keeping the Law in all its detail. ***fasting***. The Pharisees did not eat from 6:00 a.m. to 6:00 p.m. on Mondays and Thursdays as an act of piety.

2:19–20 For the very poor there were few events to break the monotony and tedium of their lives. Marriage was one such occasion. Rather than go on a honeymoon, a Jewish couple stayed with their friends for a week-long feast during which everyone was released from all religious obligations including fasting. ***the bridegroom will be taken from them***. An ominous note predicting Jesus' death.

2:21–22 Jesus uses two more mini–parables to make his point. His new way is not compatible with the old way of the Pharisees, any more than one can sew new cloth on old and not have it pull apart. Nor can one put new wine in an old, dry wineskin and not have the young, vigorous wine burst out.

2:23 *Sabbath*. The seventh day of the week (Saturday) which begins Friday at sunset and ends Saturday at sunset. The Fourth Commandment is to rest from all labor on the Sabbath (Ex 20:8–11). ***pick some heads of grain***. It was permissible for hungry travellers to pluck and eat grain from a field (Dt 23:25). The issue is not stealing. What the Pharisees objected to was the "work" this involved. Reaping was one of the 39 categories of work forbidden on the Sabbath.

2:24 *unlawful*. The "law" they cite refers to those customs and regulations (both written and oral) that the Pharisees zealously guarded. Jesus did not take issue with Exodus 34:21, but with the rigid interpretation given it.

2:26 *In the days of Abiathar*. In fact, it was Abiathar's father, Ahimelech, who was High Priest when this incident occurred (see 1Sa 21:1–6). This may be a scribal error, though it is probably just a reference to a general section of Scripture. ***ate the consecrated bread***. David did what was unlawful (Ex 25:30; Nu 4:7), providing a precedent that human need can supercede law.

2:27 So many Sabbath laws had evolved that the Sabbath had become a burden, not a blessing. Jesus seeks to restore the original meaning of the Sabbath. This is one of the few verses found only in Mark.

2:28 *Son of Man*. This is Jesus' favorite title for himself. In the Aramaic that Jesus spoke it would not have been a title at all, but simply a common expression meaning "a man." But it was also true that this phrase was used as a Messianic title in Daniel 7 and in the apocryphal Book of Enoch (written around 70 B.C.). So by using this rather colorless, vague title to characterize himself (which nonetheless had Messianic connotations), Jesus would be able to define it in his own way and say, "This is the kind of Messiah I am."

3:1–6 In the final incident in these five confrontation stories (2:1–3:6), the religious leaders come to a conclusion about Jesus: he is dangerous, and so must die.

3:2 *they watched him closely*. By this time the religious leaders no longer questioned Jesus. Now they simply watched to see if his actions betrayed a disregard for law. ***if he would heal on the Sabbath***. The issue is not healing, but whether Jesus would do so on the Sabbath in defiance of the oral tradition, which allowed healing only if there was danger to life. Jesus could have waited until the next day to heal this long-paralyzed hand.

3:5 *anger/deeply distressed*. Jesus felt strongly about the injustice of a system that sacrificed the genuine needs of people for the traditions of men, all in the name of piety. ***stubborn hearts***. Just as the religious leaders have come to a conclusion about him (see 3:6), he has come to understand them. Their problem is that their hearts (the center of their beings) have calcified. ***Stretch out your hand***. Just as he deliberately declared the paralytic's sins forgiven (knowing that this was blasphemy to the teachers of the law), here he deliberately heals on the Sabbath (knowing that this too was anathema to his critics).

3:6 *Herodians*. A political group made up of influential Jewish sympathizers of King Herod. They were normally despised by the Pharisees, who considered them traitors (for working with Rome) and irreligious (unclean as a result of their association with Gentiles). However, the Pharisees had no power to kill Jesus. Only the civil authority can do this and hence the collaboration.

UNIT 5 Crowds Follow Jesus/The Twelve Appointed/Jesus and Beelzebub/ Jesus' Mother and Brothers

Mark 3:7-35

Questions

Crowds Follow Jesus

⁷Jesus withdrew with his disciples to the lake, and a large crowd from Galilee followed. ⁸When they heard all he was doing, many people came to him from Judea, Jerusalem, Idumea, and the regions across the Jordan and around Tyre and Sidon. ⁹Because of the crowd he told his disciples to have a small boat ready for him, to keep the people from crowding him. ¹⁰For he had healed many, so that those with diseases were pushing forward to touch him. ¹¹Whenever the evil^g spirits saw him, they fell down before him and cried out, "You are the Son of God." ¹²But he gave them strict orders not to tell who he was.

The Appointing of the Twelve Apostles

¹³Jesus went up on a mountainside and called to him those he wanted, and they came to him. ¹⁴He appointed twelve—designating them apostles^h—that they might be with him and that he might send them out to preach ¹⁵and to have authority to drive out demons. ¹⁶These are the twelve he appointed: Simon (to whom he gave the name Peter); ¹⁷James son of Zebedee and his brother John (to them he gave the name Boanerges, which means Sons of Thunder); ¹⁸Andrew, Philip, Bartholomew, Matthew, Thomas, James son of Alphaeus, Thaddaeus, Simon the Zealot ¹⁹and Judas Iscariot, who betrayed him.

Jesus and Beelzebub

²⁰Then Jesus entered a house, and again a crowd gathered, so that he and his disciples were not even able to eat. ²¹When his family heard about this, they went to take charge of him, for they said, "He is out of his mind."
²²And the teachers of the law who came down from Jerusalem said, "He is possessed by Beelzebubⁱ! By the prince of demons he is driving out demons."

OPEN: 1. What is the largest crowd of which you were a part: Political rally? Protest march? Concert? Opening day at a new mall? Times Square on New Year's Eve? Church conference? Ball game? **2.** What was your first business venture and who were your partners?

DIG: 1. From how far away were people traveling to see and hear Jesus (see notes and a Bible map)? If you were there, what would have motivated you to come? What motives would have pleased Jesus? Why? What commitment did the crowds have to him? **2.** How might the events of verses 7-12 lead Jesus to choose the Twelve? Why that many (or that few)? What is their purpose? **3.** Why such ordinary guys and not people with clout? Is this any way to run a campaign? **4.** In verse 20, why was Jesus' family worried about him? What type of conversation must they have had before they decided to get him? **5.** What is the significance of where these Pharisees were from? What tensions might these uneducated people feel when they hear what these respected, educated leaders say about Jesus? **6.** How do Jesus' parables answer the charge? How do they relate to verse 29? **7.** What did the crowd expect in verses 31-32? What did Jesus say is the basis for a family relationship with him? Is doing God's will an *action* or a *belief* (see Lk 6:46; Jn 6:29)? How so?

[Scripture and questions continued on page 22]

---

^g11 Greek *unclean*; also in verse 30   ^h14 Some manuscripts do not have *designating them apostles.*   ⁱ22 Greek *Beezeboul* or *Beelzeboul*

Notes

3:7–35 In 1:16-45 Mark described the enthusiasm with which the crowds greeted Jesus. In 2:1–3:6 he described, in contrast, the hostility the religious leaders had toward Jesus. In this section he further differentiates the reactions to Jesus. Two groups are for him: the crowds (3:7–12) and the disciples (3:13–19). Two groups are against him: his family (3:20–21; 31–35) and the teachers of the law (3:22–30).

3:7–12 In a day when there was little effective medicine, the crowds flock to Jesus because he was a successful healer and because he had the power to cast out demons (see 1:28).

3:8 They came from near (Galilee) and far: from the north (Tyre and Sidon), the south (Idumea), and the East (the region across the Jordan was called the Peraea). (To the west was the sea.) They came from Jewish and from Gentile regions. They came from the country regions (Galilee) and from the heart of the nation (Jerusalem).

3:9 The lake provided a barrier against the crowds as well as a natural amplifier for his voice.

3:11–12 Once again the evil spirits correctly identify him ("the Son of God"). They name him because in ancient times it was thought that knowing a person's true name gave you the ability to control that person. But in a vindication of this title, Jesus exerts power over these evil forces and silences them, lest they stir up the crowds to follow him as the Messiah who will lead them in revolt against Rome.

3:13–19 In contrast to the crowds who came to have their needs met, Jesus selected ("called to him," "appointed," or "designated") twelve to be his disciples.

3:14–15 *apostles*. Ambassadors commissioned to go out in his name. *twelve*. There were twelve tribes in Israel. Jesus and his disciples will inaugurate the new Israel.

3:16–19 Peter's name heads each list of the apostles; Judas' is always last. There are two (possibly three) sets of brothers and several sets of friends. Some of these men are strong-willed and impetuous (the Sons of Thunder, who want to consume a village with fire in Lk 9:51–56);

some are so invisible they are known only from the lists (e.g. Thaddaeus). There are two natural enemies: the pro–government tax collector Matthew (Levi) and the anti–government guerrilla Simon.

3:20–21, 31–35 For the first time, Jesus' family is heard from, though in a surprising role. Whether out of good motives (they are concerned that he is not able to take care of himself with the crowds constantly pressing him, v.20) or out of misunderstanding (he is acting strange, v.21), his family wants to stop Jesus' ministry. *they went*. They undertook the 30-mile journey from Nazareth to Capernaum. *take charge of him*. Take him home by force (see 6:17, where the same word is translated "arrested"). *out of his mind*. Lit., "he is beside himself." His family concludes that he is suffering from some sort of ecstatic, religiously-induced mental illness.

3:22–30 Sandwiched into the story of his family is this account of how the teachers of the law explain Jesus' power. This is the first of several occasions in which Mark places a story between the beginning and the end of another story. In this way the two stories amplify and explain one another.

3:22 *came down from Jerusalem*. To go from Jerusalem in the south to Galilee in the north you go *down* (because Jerusalem stood at an elevation of 2,400 feet above sea level, while the Sea of Galilee was 600 feet below sea level). *He is possessed by Beelzebub*. To be possessed by this demon is to be controlled and empowered by him, which is how the teachers of the law explained Jesus' miracles. They cannot deny his healing and exorcism, and since they know they are God's representatives (and Jesus is not one of them), the only other source of such power is Satan. The charge that Jesus is a sorcerer was found frequently in Jewish literature until the modern age. *Beelzebub* is probably a slang expression for a demon-prince, meaning something like "The Lord of Dung."

3:23–27 Jesus begins by pointing out the flaw in their argument: the power of Satan cannot be used to undo the power of Satan. Then by means of three brief parables he drives home his point. A kingdom (or even a house) that wars against itself

[Notes continued on page 23]   21

Mark 3:7-35, continued

²³So Jesus called them and spoke to them in parables: "How can Satan drive out Satan? ²⁴If a kingdom is divided against itself, that kingdom cannot stand. ²⁵If a house is divided against itself, that house cannot stand. ²⁶And if Satan opposes himself and is divided, he cannot stand; his end has come. ²⁷In fact, no one can enter a strong man's house and carry off his possessions unless he first ties up the strong man. Then he can rob his house. ²⁸I tell you the truth, all the sins and blasphemies of men will be forgiven them. ²⁹But whoever blasphemes against the Holy Spirit will never be forgiven; he is guilty of an eternal sin."

³⁰He said this because they were saying, "He has an evil spirit."

Jesus' Mother and Brothers

³¹Then Jesus' mother and brothers arrived. Standing outside, they sent someone in to call him. ³²A crowd was sitting around him, and they told him, "Your mother and brothers are outside looking for you."

³³"Who are my mother and my brothers?" he asked.

³⁴Then he looked at those seated in a circle around him and said, "Here are my mother and my brothers! ³⁵Whoever does God's will is my brother and sister and mother."

Questions

REFLECT: 1. How can you tell if a person's mistaken ideas about Jesus stem from misunderstanding or a hard heart? 2. How has Jesus plundered Satan's kingdom in your life? 3. What would be true of a kingdom where the king viewed his subjects as his brothers and sisters? How does that reflect Jesus' relationship with you? 4. Of the responses to Jesus in this chapter (3:6, 8, 21, 22, 34-35), which best describes your relationship to him now? Why?

Notes, continued

will fall. Furthermore, he has used his power to bind Satan ("the strong man"), as demonstrated by the fact that he is undoing Satan's works every time he heals or casts out a demon.

3:28–29 Jesus ends by stating that all manner of sin will be forgiven ("all the sins and blasphemies of men"). However, in order for forgiveness to be given it must be requested. And the teachers of the law are so blind (their hearts are hard, 3:5) that they do not notice the blasphemy in their calling Jesus (who is God's son) a tool of Satan (who is the prince of demons). Thus it would never occur to them to ask for forgiveness. To **blaspheme against the Holy Spirit** is to resist the Spirit's convicting work and thus not to see the sin, and so fail to ask for forgiveness. Anxiety about whether one has committed "an eternal sin" is the very demonstration that one is still open to the convicting work of the Spirit. Jesus warns his critics not to be guilty of the very thing they accused him of in the story of the paralytic (2:7)!

3:30 The way the Greek is phrased here indicates that the teachers of the law had a callous and fixed attitude of mind.

3:31–32 The family's assessment that Jesus is "out of his mind" is a milder version of the claim by the teachers of the law that "he is possessed by Beelzebub." At this point the family arrives to "take charge" of Jesus (this is not a friendly visit). They find him surrounded by the crowd (v.32). Not wanting to confront him in that setting, they send someone to call him out.

3:33 Jesus' question is rhetorical. He does not expect an answer.

3:34–35 Jesus gives a new definition of family. Kinship is not a matter of heredity, it is a matter of spirit; i.e., doing God's will (which his natural family is not doing by trying to stop his ministry). Eventually his family will move from doubt to faith (see Jn 19:25–27; Ac 1:14; 1Co 15:7).

UNIT 6 The Parable of the Sower

Mark 4:1-20

The Parable of the Sower

4 Again Jesus began to teach by the lake. The crowd that gathered around him was so large that he got into a boat and sat in it out on the lake, while all the people were along the shore at the water's edge. ²He taught them many things by parables, and in his teaching said: ³"Listen! A farmer went out to sow his seed. ⁴As he was scattering the seed, some fell along the path, and the birds came and ate it up. ⁵Some fell on rocky places, where it did not have much soil. It sprang up quickly, because the soil was shallow. ⁶But when the sun came up, the plants were scorched, and they withered because they had no root. ⁷Other seed fell among thorns, which grew up and choked the plants, so that they did not bear grain. ⁸Still other seed fell on good soil. It came up, grew and produced a crop, multiplying thirty, sixty, or even a hundred times."

⁹Then Jesus said, "He who has ears to hear, let him hear."

¹⁰When he was alone, the Twelve and the others around him asked him about the parables. ¹¹He told them, "The secret of the kingdom of God has been given to you. But to those on the outside everything is said in parables ¹²so that,

" 'they may be ever seeing but never perceiving,
and ever hearing but never understanding;
otherwise they might turn and be forgiven!'¹ "

¹³Then Jesus said to them, "Don't you understand this parable? How then will you understand any parable? ¹⁴The farmer sows the word. ¹⁵Some people are like seed along the path, where the word is sown. As soon as they hear it, Satan comes and takes away the word that was sown in them. ¹⁶Others, like seed sown on rocky places, hear the word and at once receive it with joy. ¹⁷But since they have no root, they last only a short time. When trouble or persecution comes because of the word, they quickly fall away. ¹⁸Still others, like seed sown among thorns, hear the word; ¹⁹but the worries of this life, the deceitfulness of wealth and the desires for other things come in and choke the word, making it unfruitful. ²⁰Others, like seed sown on good soil, hear the word, accept it, and produce a crop—thirty, sixty or even a hundred times what was sown."

Questions

OPEN: 1. Who told you the best stories when you were a kid? What made them memorable? 2. What experience (if any) have you had farming or gardening? Do houseplants tend to thrive or die under your care?

DIG: 1. Some see essentially two, typically four, and even six kinds of soil here (see notes). Which types of soil can you identify? What kind of growth occurred in each soil type? 2. How might this crowd have responded to such a parable? How are the parables like a spiritual "hearing test"? What blocks understanding? What distinguishes those who are told "the secret of the kingdom" from those "outside"? 3. Why does the word not take root at all in some people? What causes the second plant to wither? What three things choked off the third plant? How do you account for the miracle crop? 4. In the context of chapter 3, how does this parable explain the various responses to Jesus? 5. What modern analogy would you use to explain this parable to city kids who have never seen a farm?

REFLECT: 1. Which soil would best describe your response to the gospel when you first heard it? What kind of crop have you been producing lately? How does one become the good soil? 2. In your circle of acquaintances, which kind of "soil" do you often see in their hearts? 3. What does this parable teach you about failure and success in evangelism? Should we sow the gospel indiscriminately? Why or why not? How can we encourage people to truly hear the gospel when many believe they have "heard it all before"?

---

¹12 Isaiah 6:9,10

24

Notes

4:1–20 The emphasis in the so–called parable of the sower is really on the soils. The four soils represent the four types of responses to Jesus seen thus far in this account of Jesus' ministry.

4:2 *parables*. Comparisons that draw upon common experience in order to teach about kingdom realities. These metaphors or analogies are often presented in story form; they draw upon the known to explain the unknown. They are often strange or vivid, forcing the hearer to think about their meaning.

4:3 *Listen!* Pay attention! There is more to this story than appears at first. Think about this or you will get it wrong. *sow his seeds*. In Palestine, farmers sowed their seeds first, scattering them by hand, and then they plowed.

4:4 *the path*. The soil of the pathways was so packed down that seed could not penetrate the soil and so germinate. The birds came along and ate up this seed on the surface of the ground.

4:5–6 *rocky places*. Some soil covered a limestone base a few inches beneath the surface. Seed that fell here would germinate but it would not last, since a proper root system could not develop.

4:7 *thorns*. In other places, there were the roots of weeds. When the seed grew up, so did the weeds, which invariably stunted the growth of the good seed. Although it lived, such seed would not bear fruit.

4:8 *good soil*. However, some of the seed did fall where it was intended. *thirty, sixty or even a hundred times*. The normal yield for a Palestinian field is seven and a half times what is sown, while ten times is an especially good harvest. This is where the emphasis in the parable lies: not with the unproductive soil, but with the miracle crop.

4:9 Jesus urges his hearers to ponder his parable. Part of a parable's power lies in the fact that people must reflect on it in order to understand it. The question is: what topic does this story from ordinary life provide insight into?

4:11–12 At first reading, this may appear to be saying that parables are designed to obscure the truth. In fact, this simply states (with some irony) what is a fact: some understand and some do not. The teachers of the law, for example, see Jesus' miracles and hear Jesus' teaching and yet they ascribe his power to Satan (3:22). They see but do not perceive. *the secret*. A secret in the NT is something which was previously unknown but has now been revealed to all who will hear. *the kingdom of God*. This is what Jesus' parables in this section are all about. This is the interpretive key (see 1:14–15). *has been given you*. Not even the disciples who have been given "the secret" perceive fully what is going on (v.13). So, to be "given the secret" must mean something like "called to follow Jesus." *those on the outside*. The point here is that God calls some to perform a particular task, namely, to spread his kingdom (see 3:13–15). *might turn and be forgiven*. In order to be forgiven, people must repent (turn). In order to repent, they must understand their true situation.

4:13–20 This is the only parable that Jesus explains in Mark's Gospel. This fact, coupled with its length (20 verses when most stories occupy 10 verses or less), indicates how important this parable is for Mark. By it, he helps the reader understand the four types of response to Jesus seen thus far in the Gospel. In this parable, it becomes clear that only one response (that of the Twelve) will bear fruit for the kingdom.

4:15 Some, like the teachers of the law, are so hardened that the seed of the word never even penetrates. *Satan*. The teachers of the law have charged Jesus with being dominated by Satan when, in fact, it turns out that they are the ones under his influence!

4:16–17 Others, like the crowds, are superficially attracted to Jesus. They like what he can give them, but their commitment is not deep (see 3:7–12). It will fall away as soon as there is any hint of persecution.

4:18–19 Still others, like his family, allow the wrong concerns to squeeze out the newly growing plant (see 3:20–21, 31–35; 6:1–6). *making it unfruitful*. The weeds do not kill the plant, but they do prevent it from bringing forth fruit.

4:20 But in the end, some, like the Twelve, will reproduce abundantly (see 3:13–19). *thirty, sixty or even a hundred times*. In this parable there are three types of unproductive soil (hard, rocky, weed-filled) and also, so it would appear, three types of productive soil (that bearing 30-, 60-, and 100-fold). Or looked at another way, there are only two kinds of soil: unproductive and productive.

UNIT 7 Lamp on a Stand/Parable of Growing Seed/Mustard Seed/Jesus Calms the Storm

Mark 4:21-41

A Lamp on a Stand

[21]He said to them, "Do you bring in a lamp to put it under a bowl or a bed? Instead, don't you put it on its stand? [22]For whatever is hidden is meant to be disclosed, and whatever is concealed is meant to be brought out into the open. [23]If anyone has ears to hear, let him hear."

[24]"Consider carefully what you hear," he continued. "With the measure you use, it will be measured to you—and even more. [25]Whoever has will be given more; whoever does not have, even what he has will be taken from him."

The Parable of the Growing Seed

[26]He also said, "This is what the kingdom of God is like. A man scatters seed on the ground. [27]Night and day, whether he sleeps or gets up, the seed sprouts and grows, though he does not know how. [28]All by itself the soil produces grain—first the stalk, then the head, then the full kernel in the head. [29]As soon as the grain is ripe, he puts the sickle to it, because the harvest has come."

The Parable of the Mustard Seed

[30]Again he said, "What shall we say the kingdom of God is like, or what parable shall we use to describe it? [31]It is like a mustard seed, which is the smallest seed you plant in the ground. [32]Yet when planted, it grows and becomes the largest of all garden plants, with such big branches that the birds of the air can perch in its shade."

[33]With many similar parables Jesus spoke the word to them, as much as they could understand. [34]He did not say anything to them without using a parable. But when he was alone with his own disciples, he explained everything.

Jesus Calms the Storm

[35]That day when evening came, he said to his disciples, "Let us go over to the other side." [36]Leaving the crowd behind, they took him along, just as he was, in the boat. There were also other boats with him. [37]A furious squall came up, and the waves broke over the boat, so that it was nearly swamped. [38]Jesus was in the stern, sleeping on a cushion. The disciples woke him and said to him, "Teacher, don't you care if we drown?"

[39]He got up, rebuked the wind and said to the waves, "Quiet! Be still!" Then the wind died down and it was completely calm.

[40]He said to his disciples, "Why are you so afraid? Do you still have no faith?"

[41]They were terrified and asked each other, "Who is this? Even the wind and the waves obey him!"

Questions

OPEN: 1. As a child, what "big dream" did you have about what you would be when you grew up? **2.** What is your favorite TV game show? Do you try to figure out the questions, or just wait for the answers? Why?

DIG: 1. If Jesus is the lamp (v.21), what is he revealing (see also vv.11-12)? **2.** What is the secret of receiving more from Jesus? **3.** In verses 26-29, what part (if any) do people play in the growing kingdom? How does this parable complement the one in verses 3-20? **4.** What does the contrast between the seed and the bush teach about the kingdom (vv.30-32)? **5.** What do all of these parables show about God's kingdom? **6.** If you could put yourself in the boat in verses 35-41, what emotions would you feel as this storm raged on and on? What did the disciples want from Jesus? How do you picture their faces in verses 39-41? Which would frighten you more—the storm or Jesus? **7.** What was Jesus showing them about himself in all this?

REFLECT: 1. How do you react to Jesus when he seems to be asleep in your life? **2.** In terms of the light of Christ that you shed, are you a 20-, 60-, 100-, or 200-watt light bulb? Or burned out? Why? **3.** Does knowing that the growth of the kingdom is ultimately in God's hands cause you to rest or to work more? Why? **4.** Taking verses 28 and 31 personally, at what stage is the kingdom in your life now: Still a seed? Sprouting? Outgrowing the "weeds"? Producing a harvest? **5.** What hope do these parables give you when you feel that you, your church, or your work for Christ is insignificant?

Notes

4:21-32 These four parables are used by Matthew and Luke in quite different ways in their Gospels (see Mt 5:15; 10:26; 7:2; 25:29; Lk 8:16–18; 6:38; 10:26). The parables teach that the kingdom of God (like Jesus' Messiahship) will have a hidden period, but one day it will be revealed for what it really is.

4:21-23 This parable is a comment on the secrecy motif introduced in verse 11. The kingdom of God is not meant to be hidden but to be revealed. **lamp**. A pottery vessel filled with olive oil. **bowl**. A basket which could hold about one peck. **bed**. The couch on which people reclined while eating.

4:24-25 Again in verse 24, the hearers are warned to listen carefully (see vv. 9, 23). Then they are told a riddle that emphasizes that there are consequences to how they hear Jesus. Those who do not hear nor heed his words will miss out on God's kingdom, while those who grasp what is happening will grow in their understanding of the emerging kingdom.

4:26-29 This is the only parable unique to Mark. It shows how the seed falling into the good soil (the fourth kind) grows into abundant fruit. Such an insignificant act as sowing seed yields, in the fullness of time, an incredible harvest.

4:30-32 The final parable contrasts the seeming insignificance of a tiny mustard seed with the luxurious plant it becomes. So, too, the seeming insignificance of Jesus' ministry: he was a free-lance rabbi with twelve largely non-descript disciples. Yet one day his work will blossom into the magnificent kingdom of God. **mustard seed**. To the Jew, the mustard tree was proverbial for having the smallest seed. Along the Lake of Galilee, mustard shrubs grew to 8 or 10 feet. The shade they provided, along with the tasty black seeds, attracted flocks of birds.

4:33 as much as they could understand. This reinforces the fact that the intention was not to veil his message by means of parables, but to reveal it. The problem was the understanding level of his hearers.

4:35-5:43 Mark begins a new section. In 1:14-4:34, he explored various responses to Jesus. Despite differing reactions to Jesus, everyone seemed to regard him as a rabbi: He taught with authority (e.g., 1:27), he healed effectively (e.g., 1:34), and he cast out demons easily (e.g., 1:39). In other words, he did what other rabbis did (or tried to do), except that he

was exceptionally good at it. In these four stories, a whole new side of Jesus is revealed: Mark unveils the awesome *power* of Jesus. The disciples see that he has authority over the very elements (4:35-41); over the most extreme case of possession by evil (5:1-20); over long-term, seemingly incurable disease (4:24-34); and even over death itself (4:21-24, 36-43). No rabbi had *this* kind of power. Whoever Jesus was, he went beyond normal categories.

4:35 That day. This story comes at the end of a day of teaching by the lake (see 4:1). **when evening came**. This voyage begins as the sun is setting.

4:37 A furious squall. The Sea of Galilee was a deep, fresh water lake, 13 miles long and 8 miles wide. Fierce winds blew into this bowl-shaped sea, creating savage and unpredictable storms.

4:38 sleeping. In the OT, sleeping peacefully is a sign of trust in the power of God (e.g., Ps 4:8). The fact that Jesus was asleep during a storm is also a sign of his exhaustion from a day of teaching. **Teacher**. This is who they understood Jesus to be: a rabbi. **don't you care if we drown?** They wake Jesus up so that he can help them bail out the boat since it was about to be swamped (v.37). As their later response indicates (v.41), they had no expectation that he would have any power over the storm.

4:39 Instead of bailing, Jesus commands the wind and the waves to be still and so they are. He has power over the very elements—in the same way that God does (see Ps 65:7; 106:9). **Be still!** This is literally, "Be muzzled!" as if the storm were some wild beast needing to be subdued.

4:40 afraid. Some of the disciples were fishermen who knew how serious their peril was. However, once Jesus displays his power, their physical fear turns to something else.

4:41 terrified. Terror replaced fear. This is what is felt in the presence of an unknown force or power. **Who is this?** This is the key question in Mark's Gospel. The congregation in the synagogue wondered about this (1:27). The religious leaders asked this question (2:7; 3:22). Now his disciples discover that they do not understood who he is. Only the readers of the Gospel (1:1), God (1:11), and the demons (1:24, 35) know his true identity. The rest of Mark describes how the disciples discover his true nature.

UNIT 8   Healing of a Demon-Possessed Man

Mark 5:1-20

The Healing of a Demon-possessed Man

5 They went across the lake to the region of the Gerasenes.[k] [2]When Jesus got out of the boat, a man with an evil[l] spirit came from the tombs to meet him. [3]This man lived in the tombs, and no one could bind him any more, not even with a chain. [4]For he had often been chained hand and foot, but he tore the chains apart and broke the irons on his feet. No one was strong enough to subdue him. [5]Night and day among the tombs and in the hills he would cry out and cut himself with stones.

[6]When he saw Jesus from a distance, he ran and fell on his knees in front of him. [7]He shouted at the top of his voice, "What do you want with me, Jesus, Son of the Most High God? Swear to God that you won't torture me!" [8]For Jesus had said to him, "Come out of this man, you evil spirit!"

[9]Then Jesus asked him, "What is your name?"

"My name is Legion," he replied, "for we are many." [10]And he begged Jesus again and again not to send them out of the area.

[11]A large herd of pigs was feeding on the nearby hillside. [12]The demons begged Jesus, "Send us among the pigs; allow us to go into them." [13]He gave them permission, and the evil spirits came out and went into the pigs. The herd, about two thousand in number, rushed down the steep bank into the lake and were drowned.

[14]Those tending the pigs ran off and reported this in the town and countryside, and the people went out to see what had happened. [15]When they came to Jesus, they saw the man who had been possessed by the legion of demons, sitting there, dressed and in his right mind; and they were afraid. [16]Those who had seen it told the people what had happened to the demon-possessed man—and told about the pigs as well. [17]Then the people began to plead with Jesus to leave their region.

[18]As Jesus was getting into the boat, the man who had been demon-possessed begged to go with him. [19]Jesus did not let him, but said, "Go home to your family and tell them how much the Lord has done for you, and how he has had mercy on you." [20]So the man went away and began to tell in the Decapolis[m] how much Jesus had done for him. And all the people were amazed.

Questions

OPEN: 1. In your hometown, who was the "strange person"—the one everyone tried to avoid? Did you have any run-ins with this spooky individual? **2.** Do you like horror films and books? Why or why not?

DIG: 1. How are the disciples feeling as they cross the lake? After a ride like theirs, how would it feel to be accosted by this man in the cemetery at night? **2.** What do you learn about demons from the actions of the possessed man? **3.** How does the healing take place? What is the man like afterwards? **4.** Why do you think the people react as they do? Why were they afraid (v.15) instead of rejoicing after seeing the man "dressed and in his right mind"? What does this say about their values? **5.** What was the ethnic background of those in the Decapolis? How might that explain the charge to witness (v.19), when previously Jesus ordered silence (1:43-44)? **6.** What do you think the demoniac said to his family? **7.** What did the disciples learn about Jesus this day (4:35-5:20)?

REFLECT: 1. When have you felt like the demoniac—torn by so many conflicting voices and feelings? How did Jesus bring peace into that chaos? How do you need to hear his word of peace right now? **2.** When have you felt like the townspeople, wishing Jesus would leave because he changes things too much? **3.** When have you seen someone's livelihood ("pigs") affected by conversion to Christ? Would you be open to this happening to you or to anyone in your family? Why or why not?

---

[k]*1* Some manuscripts *Gadarenes*; other manuscripts *Gergesenes*   [l]*2* Greek *unclean*; also in verses 8 and 13   [m]*20* That is, the Ten Cities

Notes

5:1-20 Mark tells a second power story. This time Jesus confronts a man who is ravished by not one but thousands of demons. Once again he demonstrates his power by casting out this combined force of demons and healing a man whose body and personality had been overwhelmed by this evil possession. The length of this account is an indication of its importance to Mark.

5:1 *the region of the Gerasenes*. The precise location of their landing is not clear. However, it is on the other side of the lake from Capernaum (in Gentile territory) probably near the lower end of the Sea of Galilee.

5:2 *Jesus got out of the boat*. No mention is made of the disciples in this story. Given what they had been through on the lake (and the fact that they landed in a Gentile region at night in a graveyard with a nightmare-like figure howling at them), it is not surprising that only Jesus got out of the boat to face this terror. ***a man with an evil spirit***. There was wide-spread belief that demons could enter and take control of a person's body, speaking and acting through that person. First-century people lived in dread of demons (see note on 1:23). They avoided places, like cemetaries, where they were thought to dwell. ***tombs***. The ragged limestone cliffs with their caves and depressions provided natural tombs.

5:3-5 The man was a living terror: naked, physically so powerful he could not be subdued, naked, cut up and perhaps bleeding, crying out in the tombs.

5:6-9 The naming ritual begins and the demons try to master Jesus by crying out his true identity (see note 1:24). All the while Jesus is commanding the demons to leave the man (v.8). Finally, Jesus compels the demons to reveal their name (v.9). ***Son of the Most High God***. The disciples ask who Jesus is (see 4:41); the demon-filled man, with supernatural insight, points out Jesus' divine nature (see 1:11). Interestingly, this is how God was often referred to by Gentiles (see Ge 14:17-24; Da 4:17; Ps 97:9). ***Legion***. The name for a company of 6,000 Roman soldiers. The man was occupied not by one, but by a huge number of demons. This name also conveys the sense of warfare that is going on between Jesus and Satan.

5:11-13 *pigs*. This was a Gentile herd, since no Jew would raise pigs (Lev 11:1-8). This was probably a herd made up of pigs owned by various people in town.

5:14-17 The whole incident is reported to the townspeople who arrive *en masse* and there find the healed demoniac. ***they were afraid***. It might be expected that they would rejoice that this man who had terrorized them (and whom they could no longer restrain) was now healed. But instead they are fearful of Jesus who had the power to overcome the demons and destroy their town herd. ***the people began to plead with Jesus to leave***. They want no part of one who in their eyes would appear to be a powerful magician; one who regarded a single madman to be worth more than their whole town herd.

5:18-20 The focus shifts from the frightened townfolk to the grateful ex-demoniac. He wants to join Jesus' band, but is instead commanded to return home and share his story of God's mercy. ***tell***. In contrast to what Jesus said to the leper: "See that you don't tell this to anyone" (1:44), he wants this man to share the story of his healing. The difference is that the leper was Jewish and his story might cause people to think that the Messiah had come before they knew what kind of Messiah Jesus was. Gentiles, however, did not have such messianic expectations. Interestingly, what the ex-demoniac could tell them was limited. He could explain what he was like before he met Jesus, what had happened to him when he encountered Jesus, and what little he knew about Jesus. This first Gentile witness to Jesus had no theological training; he simply had an amazing story to tell by which God's nature would be revealed. ***Decapolis***. A league of ten Gentile cities patterned after the Greek way of life. This is the first of several ventures by Jesus into Gentile areas, demonstrating what Mark later points out (13:10; 14:9), that the gospel is to be preached to all nations. Mark's Roman readers would find encouragement in the fact that right from the start the Lord ministered to non-Jews like them.

UNIT 9 A Dead Girl and a Sick Woman

Mark 5:21-43

Questions

A Dead Girl and a Sick Woman

²¹When Jesus had again crossed over by boat to the other side of the lake, a large crowd gathered around him while he was by the lake. ²²Then one of the synagogue rulers, named Jairus, came there. Seeing Jesus, he fell at his feet ²³and pleaded earnestly with him, "My little daughter is dying. Please come and put your hands on her so that she will be healed and live." ²⁴So Jesus went with him.

A large crowd followed and pressed around him. ²⁵And a woman was there who had been subject to bleeding for twelve years. ²⁶She had suffered a great deal under the care of many doctors and had spent all she had, yet instead of getting better she grew worse. ²⁷When she heard about Jesus, she came up behind him in the crowd and touched his cloak, ²⁸because she thought, "If I just touch his clothes, I will be healed." ²⁹Immediately her bleeding stopped and she felt in her body that she was freed from her suffering.

³⁰At once Jesus realized that power had gone out from him. He turned around in the crowd and asked, "Who touched my clothes?"

³¹"You see the people crowding against you," his disciples answered, "and yet you can ask, 'Who touched me?'"

³²But Jesus kept looking around to see who had done it. ³³Then the woman, knowing what had happened to her, came and fell at his feet and, trembling with fear, told him the whole truth. ³⁴He said to her, "Daughter, your faith has healed you. Go in peace and be freed from your suffering."

³⁵While Jesus was still speaking, some men came from the house of Jairus, the synagogue ruler. "Your daughter is dead," they said. "Why bother the teacher any more?"

³⁶Ignoring what they said, Jesus told the synagogue ruler, "Don't be afraid; just believe."

³⁷He did not let anyone follow him except Peter, James and John the brother of James. ³⁸When they came to the home of the synagogue ruler, Jesus saw a commotion, with people crying and wailing loudly. ³⁹He went in and said to them, "Why all this commotion and wailing? The child is not dead but asleep." ⁴⁰But they laughed at him.

After he put them all out, he took the child's father and mother and the disciples who were with him, and went in where the child was. ⁴¹He took her by the hand and said to her, *"Talitha koum!"* (which means, "Little girl, I say to you, get up!"). ⁴²Immediately the girl stood up and walked around (she was twelve years old). At this they were completely astonished. ⁴³He gave strict orders not to let anyone know about this, and told them to give her something to eat.

OPEN: 1. What would you do if the phone rang, the doorbell chimed, your child called for help, and the oven alarm went off all at the same time? **2.** Have you ever touched a famous person? What did that do for you?

DIG: 1. Of all the people pressing for Jesus' attention, two get through to him in this story—how so? What do these two women have in common (see notes)? **2.** What impressions do you get of the sick woman (vv.25-26)? Since this illness made her ceremonially unclean (and thus unable to have contact with other people), what do you think it took for her to touch Jesus? **3.** Why do you think Jesus makes the sick woman reveal herself: For his sake? For her sake? How was her faith obvious to Jesus? **4.** What is the relationship (here) between faith and healing? In what ways, other than physical, was this woman healed and given new peace? **5.** What impressions do you get of Jairus (vv.22-23)? How is his situation similar to that of the sick woman? How is it different? **6.** What is Jesus' reaction to the news that the child is dead? Jairus' reaction? Why did Jesus say the child was "asleep"? What tells you (from the scene at Jairus' home) that she was indeed dead? As Jairus, what would you say to the crowd outside your house after Jesus left? **7.** What new things do the disciples learn about the power of Jesus? What do the stories in 4:35-5:43 have in common?

REFLECT: 1. What is the relationship between crisis and faith in your life? Have you been like the woman? Like Jairus? The men in verse 35? The mourners in verse 40? How so? **2.** In your experience, what is the role of faith in healing? Likewise, what is the role of touch? **3.** Where do you need Jesus' healing touch now? Who do you need to reach out and touch in Jesus' name?

Notes

5:21-43 Here Mark tells two more "power" stories that deal with "unclean" people: a bleeding woman and a dead girl. In this section, Mark once again interweaves two stories (see also 3:20-35), signifying that they are to be understood in relation to each other. Both deal with females; both are second-class citizens in the first century; both are unclean; and both are healed by faith through Jesus' touch.

5:22 synagogue rulers. The Temple in Jerusalem was the sole place for sacrifice, and was attended by many priests and officials. In contrast, synagogues were found in each town. People met there every Sabbath for worship and instruction. Synagogues were run by a committee of lay people (the rulers). **he fell at his feet**. It wasn't easy for Jairus, a community leader, to humble himself before Jesus. But concern for his girl outweighed his pride.

5:23 put your hands on her. The laying on of hands was a common practice used for ordination, for blessing, in the sacrificial ritual, and for healing.

5:25 a woman was there. She should not have been there in the crowd. Because of the nature of her illness, she was considered "unclean." If people touched her, they too would become "unclean." **subject to bleeding**. Probably hemorrhaging from the womb. In any case, any such bleeding rendered her ritually impure (see Lev 15:25-30), thus cutting her off from contact with other people, including her husband. As a result, she has to seek out Jesus in this surreptitious way.

5:26 When Luke the physician told this story (Lk 8:42-48), he dropped out this verse with its rather scathing condemnation of doctors! **the care of many doctors**. Typical cures would have included such things as carrying the ash of an ostrich egg in a certain cloth, or drinking wine mixed with rubber, alum, and garden crocuses.

5:30 power. The mysterious power of God. For the first time, Mark identifies clearly what these four stories (4:35-5:43) are all about.

5:32 Jesus insists that the person who touched him reveal herself. Her healing will not be complete without this, since her illness had not only physical but social consequences. Jesus makes it publicly known that she has been healed so that she can once again have a normal relational life (see also 1:44).

5:34 your faith has healed you. It was her faith that impelled her to reach out to Jesus—the source of healing power. The word Jesus uses to tell her that she is healed comes from the same root as the words "salvation" and "Savior." Spiritual as well as physical healing is in view here. **Go in peace**. Jesus did not mean by this "Be free from worry." This phrase means "Be complete, be whole." Each of these four incidents portrays an extreme situation in which there is no hope, and yet each ends in peace as the result of the power of Jesus (see 4:39; 5:15; 5:34; 5:42).

5:35-36 It is reported to Jairus that his daughter has died, so Jesus' help is no longer needed. Jesus might be able to heal a sick girl, but no one expected that he could do anything about a dead child. Jesus, however, counsels faith in the face of fear. This is a motif that runs through all four stories (see 4:40; 5:15,33,36).

5:38 people crying and wailing loudly. These were in all likelihood professional mourners. Even the poorest person was required to hire not less than two flutes and one wailing woman to mourn a death. They are a sign that all felt the child was dead.

5:39 The child is not dead but asleep. This is said to reassure the father. The presence of the mourners, the report of the messengers, the laughter that greeted this statement all say the same thing: the child was truly dead. Jesus uses this same expression in reference to Lazarus (Jn 11:11-15).

5:41 Talitha koum! This is Aramaic, the language of Palestine. It means, literally, "Arise, lamb" and emphasizes Jesus' compassion. Mark translates this phrase for the benefit of his Gentile readers.

5:42 Immediately. She is made fully alive and is able to walk and eat. Jesus has actually done the impossible. He has raised a person from the dead in this ultimate demonstration of his power.

5:43 strict orders not to let anyone know about this. Jesus' statement that she is asleep, not dead (v.39) makes it possible for her parents to obey his request. At this point in his ministry, if word got out that Jesus could raise people from the dead, it would cause the populace to make the wrong assumptions about him ("He is the Messiah who will lead us to victory over the Romans"), and thus frustrate his true ministry.

UNIT 10 Prophet Without Honor/Jesus Sends Out the Twelve/John the Baptist Beheaded

Mark 6:1-29

A Prophet Without Honor

6 Jesus left there and went to his hometown, accompanied by his disciples. [2]When the Sabbath came, he began to teach in the synagogue, and many who heard him were amazed.

"Where did this man get these things?" they asked. "What's this wisdom that has been given him, that he even does miracles! [3]Isn't this the carpenter? Isn't this Mary's son and the brother of James, Joseph, " Judas and Simon? Aren't his sisters here with us?" And they took offense at him.

[4]Jesus said to them, "Only in his hometown, among his relatives and in his own house is a prophet without honor." [5]He could not do any miracles there, except lay his hands on a few sick people and heal them. [6]And he was amazed at their lack of faith.

Jesus Sends Out the Twelve

Then Jesus went around teaching from village to village. [7]Calling the Twelve to him, he sent them out two by two and gave them authority over evil[o] spirits.

[8]These were his instructions: "Take nothing for the journey except a staff—no bread, no bag, no money in your belts. [9]Wear sandals but not an extra tunic. [10]Whenever you enter a house, stay there until you leave that town. [11]And if any place will not welcome you or listen to you, shake the dust off your feet when you leave, as a testimony against them."

[12]They went out and preached that people should repent. [13]They drove out many demons and anointed many sick people with oil and healed them.

John the Baptist Beheaded

[14]King Herod heard about this, for Jesus' name had become well known. Some were saying,[p] "John the Baptist has been raised from the dead, and that is why miraculous powers are at work in him."

[15]Others said, "He is Elijah."

And still others claimed, "He is a prophet, like one of the prophets of long ago."

Questions

OPEN: What childhood escapade of yours do you hear about most often when you visit family?

DIG: 1. After these four "power" miracles, what happens when Jesus goes home? Why? What do the four questions (vv.2-3) reveal? How is Jesus' ministry limited in Nazareth? **2.** In verse 7, what was the significance of the disciples' assignment for the kingdom of God? What impact would this have on the villages? On the opposition movement (3:6,22)? **3.** How is the disciples' message like that of John (1:4) and Jesus (1:14-15)? **4.** Why include this "flashback" to Herod in between sending out the disciples (vv.6-13) and their return (vv.30-31)? **5.** What drew Herod's attention to Jesus? What was the significance of Elijah and John the Baptist to the people of Jesus' day (see Mt 17:9-13)? Why might people mistake Jesus for one of them? **6.** Why does Herod jail John? What does that show about Herod? About John? About Herodias? **7.** What kind of leader do you think Herod was? What is at stake for him here? How powerful do you think he felt when he went to bed that night? What kind of soil does he represent (4:13-20)? **8.** How do the two "kings"—Jesus and Herod—differ in terms of their kingdoms, character, popularity, and use of power?

[Scripture and questions continued on page 34]

"3 Greek *Joses*, a variant of *Joseph*   [o]7 Greek *unclean*   [p]14 Some early manuscripts *He was saying*

Notes

6:1-6 Having demonstrated the great power of Jesus in the previous section, Mark now tells a story in which Jesus is unable to use this power because of the lack of faith.

6:1 *his home town*. Nazareth, which was located in the hill country of Galilee some 20 miles southwest of Capernaum. (See also Lk 4:14-30.) ***accompanied by his disciples***. This was not a private visit. Jesus arrived as a rabbi with a band of disciples. He then taught in the synagogue as would a rabbi. ***amazed***. The townspeople responded to what Jesus said in the same way as had others before them (see 1:22, 27; 2:12; 5:20).

6:2 *Where does this man get these things?* The townspeople do not deny Jesus' wisdom nor his power to do miracles. But they are puzzled as to the origin of such abilities.

6:3 "Who does this illegitimate working-class kid think he is?" is the tone of these two questions. ***carpenter***. The Greek word refers to a general craftsman who works not only in wood but also in stone and metal. ***Mary's son***. A man was never described as the son of his mother (even if she was a widow) except as an insult. The townsfolk probably heard rumors of Jesus' unusual birth and took him to be illegitimate rather than virgin-born. ***brother/sisters***. Mark names four brothers and indicates that he had sisters too. ***they took offense at him***. They could not get past his humble and familiar origins—therefore, they couldn't give credence to who he really was.

6:4 *among his own relatives and in his own home*. His family continues to oppose his ministry (see also 3:20-21). ***a prophet***. Jesus uses this term for himself. It is an accurate description, though not a complete one (see 6:14-16; 8:27-30).

6:5 The emphasis is not on Jesus' inability to do miracles (Mark has amply demonstrated that he has the power to do so), but on the hostile environment that stifles that power. To be healed, a person must have at least enough faith to come to Jesus and ask for healing.

6:6 *amazed*. Now it is Jesus' turn to be amazed. The townspeople were amazed at his teaching (6:1), but they could not get over their assumptions about him. They fault him for being ordinary ("with brothers and sisters like us"), for acting like a rabbi ("only a common laborer"), and for the supposed scandal of his birth ("Mary's son"). So they do not ask for healing. This amazes Jesus.

6:7-13 In contrast to the negative response to his power by his relatives and childhood friends, Mark shows the positive response of his disciples, who accept the challenge to go out on their own and minister in the same way as Jesus has ministered (teaching, healing, exorcism).

6:7 *he sent them out*. To go out on a ministry tour is not the idea of the Twelve. Jesus does the sending. ***two by two***. He did not send them alone—perhaps as a protection against robbers; perhaps because two witnesses have more credibility than one (see Dt 17:6); perhaps so that they will support one another as they learn to minister. ***gave them authority***. He empowers them to do battle with evil. It is in his name and power that they minister.

6:8-9 These are not universal prohibitions (see Lk 22:35-36). ***instructions***. These instructions cause the Twelve to pare down to the bare minimum. They take only the clothes on their backs and a walking stick. By faith they must trust that God will provide the rest of their needs. ***no bag***. The reference is (probably) to a begging bag commonly used by wandering priests to collect funds. ***extra tunic***. That would be used as a blanket during the chilly nights.

6:10 They are not to dishonor their host by accepting better accommodations.

6:11 Hospitality for travellers was a sacred duty. Villages not offering it were judged by the prophetic action that Jesus here commands. This is similar to what pious Jews did when they left a Gentile region and returned to Israel. They shook off the dust of the lands through which they had just travelled so as to disassociate themselves from the coming judgment against the Gentiles.

6:12-13 The Twelve performed each of the tasks that characterized Jesus' ministry: they preached repentance (1:15), they cast out demons (1:27), and they healed the sick (1:34).

[Notes continued on page 35]

Questions

[16]But when Herod heard this, he said, "John, the man I beheaded, has been raised from the dead!"

[17]For Herod himself had given orders to have John arrested, and he had him bound and put in prison. He did this because of Herodias, his brother Philip's wife, whom he had married. [18]For John had been saying to Herod, "It is not lawful for you to have your brother's wife." [19]So Herodias nursed a grudge against John and wanted to kill him. But she was not able to, [20]because Herod feared John and protected him, knowing him to be a righteous and holy man. When Herod heard John, he was greatly puzzled[q]; yet he liked to listen to him.

[21]Finally the opportune time came. On his birthday Herod gave a banquet for his high officials and military commanders and the leading men of Galilee. [22]When the daughter of Herodias came in and danced, she pleased Herod and his dinner guests.

The king said to the girl, "Ask me for anything you want, and I'll give it to you." [23]And he promised her with an oath, "Whatever you ask I will give you, up to half my kingdom."

[24]She went out and said to her mother, "What shall I ask for?"

"The head of John the Baptist," she answered.

[25]At once the girl hurried in to the king with the request: "I want you to give me right now the head of John the Baptist on a platter."

[26]The king was greatly distressed, but because of his oaths and his dinner guests, he did not want to refuse her. [27]So he immediately sent an executioner with orders to bring John's head. The man went, beheaded John in the prison, [28]and brought back his head on a platter. He presented it to the girl, and she gave it to her mother. [29]On hearing of this, John's disciples came and took his body and laid it in a tomb.

REFLECT: 1. Like Jesus' reception from his hometown and family, has familiarity with Jesus prevented you from really seeing who he is? What helps you to get a fresh look? 2. How does your family react to your faith in Christ? How does that affect you? 3. Where has God sent you to tell about the kingdom? How is it going? 4. When have you felt like Herod—attracted to the truth, but afraid to follow through with it? What happened? In contrast, how might you grow in reflecting John's courage? 5. Like Herod, when have you made a rash statement that you later regretted? Is it ever right to go back on a vow or to fail to keep a promise? When have you done so? 6. Whom do you know who is struggling with the truth and is perplexed—much like Herod? How can you reach out to them?

[q]20 Some early manuscripts *he did many things*

Notes, continued

6:14-29 In a parenthetical flashback, Mark describes how John the Baptist died at the hands of Herod. This account is sandwiched between the sending out of the Twelve (vv.7-13) and their return (v.30). This is the only story in Mark in which Jesus is not the central figure. In this passage, the relative powerlessness of Herod (who in reality held all the political power) is contrasted to the great power of Jesus (who had no official status at all). Two kings and two kingdoms are contrasted. Likewise, two banquets are contrasted (vv.39-44).

6:14-16 The issue once again is: Who is Jesus? (See also 1:27, 2:7; 4:41.) Three answers are proposed. He is John the Baptist come back from the dead (the answer Herod opts for in his guilt); he is Elijah (the forerunner of the Messiah); or he is a new prophet. **King Herod**. Herod Antipas was the ruler of the Roman provinces of Galilee and Peraea from 4 B.C. to A.D. 39. He was the son of Herod the Great, the Jewish ruler who ordered the slaughter of the babies at the time of Jesus' birth. Herod Antipas was not, in fact, the "King." When he went to Rome some years later to request this title, his power was taken away and he was banished. Herod is pretending to be King when, in fact, the real King of Israel (Jesus) is largely unrecognized. **Elijah**. The Jews felt that when Elijah returned as foretold in Malachi 3:1 and 4:5-6, their deliverance from Rome was near.

6:18 *It is not lawful...* According to Leviticus 18:16 and 20:21, it was not lawful for a man to marry his brother's wife while that brother was still alive. Herod divorced the Arabian Princess Aretas to marry Herodias who was his niece (the daughter of his half-brother) and his sister-in-law (the wife of a different brother).

6:21 *the opportune time*. Herodias was plotting a way to kill John (v.19) because of his criticism of her marriage. ***a banquet***. The sparseness of the lifestyle of the Twelve (vv. 8-11) would have contrasted greatly with the opulence of Herod's birthday party.

6:22 *the daughter of Herodias*. Herodias' teenage daughter (from her first marriage), whose name is Salome (according to Josephus the Jewish historian). ***danced***. For a princess to dance publicly before an audience of drunken men was considered most shameful. Her dance was undoubtedly highly sensual (although there is no historical evidence that it involved the seven veils mentioned in dramatized versions of this event). ***his dinner guests***. These are the leading men of the nation (v.21). They contrast with the common folk among whom the ministry of the Twelve took place (vv.12-13). ***Ask me for anything you want...*** Herodias succeeds in manipulating Herod by exploiting his lust, his drunkenness, and his tendency to show off. This is the opportunity she has been waiting for (see vv.19-20).

6:25 *the head of John the Baptist on a platter*. This was a gruesome act: serving John's head on a platter as if it were another course in the banquet.

6:27 There are two passion stories in Mark. The death of John the Baptist is the first. It sets the stage for the second: the passion and death of Jesus.

UNIT 11   Jesus Feeds the Five Thousand/ Jesus Walks on Water

Mark 6:30-56

Jesus Feeds the Five Thousand

³⁰The apostles gathered around Jesus and reported to him all they had done and taught. ³¹Then, because so many people were coming and going that they did not even have a chance to eat, he said to them, "Come with me by yourselves to a quiet place and get some rest."

³²So they went away by themselves in a boat to a solitary place. ³³But many who saw them leaving recognized them and ran on foot from all the towns and got there ahead of them. ³⁴When Jesus landed and saw a large crowd, he had compassion on them, because they were like sheep without a shepherd. So he began teaching them many things.

³⁵By this time it was late in the day, so his disciples came to him. "This is a remote place," they said, "and it's already very late. ³⁶Send the people away so they can go to the surrounding countryside and villages and buy themselves something to eat."

³⁷But he answered, "You give them something to eat."

They said to him, "That would take eight months of a man's wages'! Are we to go and spend that much on bread and give it to them to eat?"

³⁸"How many loaves do you have?" he asked. "Go and see."

When they found out, they said, "Five—and two fish."

³⁹Then Jesus directed them to have all the people sit down in groups on the green grass. ⁴⁰So they sat down in groups of hundreds and fifties. ⁴¹Taking the five loaves and the two fish and looking up to heaven, he gave thanks and broke the loaves. Then he gave them to his disciples to set before the people. He also divided the two fish among them all. ⁴²They all ate and were satisfied, ⁴³and the disciples picked up twelve basketfuls of broken pieces of bread and fish. ⁴⁴The number of the men who had eaten was five thousand.

[Scripture and questions continued on page 38]

Questions

OPEN: 1. After a busy day, how do you like to unwind? 2. How big was the largest group you've ever had over for a meal? What did you serve?

DIG: 1. Why did Jesus decide to take the disciples away? What happened as soon as they left? How did Jesus view the resulting crowd, and why? 2. How did the disciples and Jesus differ in the way they viewed the problem? How would you have felt about this intrusion? 3. What emotional concerns and follow-up questions might have been expressed by the disciples in verse 37? Why do they resist Jesus' suggestion (or command) to give the 5,000 something to eat? 4. What would you feel as a disciple when you gathered the leftovers? What was the purpose of doing so? (If God can multiply food, why save the scraps?) 5. How does Jesus' "dinner party" compare with Herod's (6:21-29)? What does this story imply about Jesus' identity? His mission? 6. What allusions do you see here between Jesus and Moses (see notes)? 7. After their frustrating day (vs.45-47), what new problem do the disciples encounter? How would you react in their place? 8. What is the significance of Jesus' walking on the water and his response to their terror (see Isa 43:1-3; 44:8)? How do you think the disciples understood it? 9. What should they have perceived in the "lesson of the loaves" that would have prepared them for this? Who is he revealing himself to be? Why is he doing it this way, rather than telling them directly? 10. How do the crowds (vv.53-56) view him?

'37 Greek *take two hundred denarii*

Notes

6:30-8:30 Mark begins his third major section. In the first section (1:14-4:34), the disciples (and others) view Jesus as an exceptionally gifted teacher. In section two (4:35-6:29), Jesus is shown to be a prophet of amazing power. Here in section three, he is discovered to be the Messiah (8:27-30). Thus the disciples' understanding of Jesus continues to unfold. In this section there are two parallel cycles of stories. The point is made that it will take a miracle from Jesus to heal the hardened hearts of the Twelve so that they can see who he really is—or at least understand as much as they can prior to his death and resurrection. Cycle one (6:30-7:37) begins with the feeding of the 5,000 and ends with the healing of a deaf and dumb man. Cycle two (8:1-26) begins with the feeding of the 4,000 and ends with the healing of a blind man. In both cycles, the reader is shown the inability of the disciples to understand what is happening. It is as if they are deaf, dumb, and blind.

6:30 The Twelve return from their mission and report to the Lord what took place in their attempt at independent ministry. **apostles**. This is the only time this term is used in Mark. Here it is not so much a title as a description of what they have just done. An apostle is "one who is sent," and they have just completed the missionary work the Lord sent them out to do (v.7).

6:31 get some rest. It is Jesus who insists on rest—even though the crowds are there with all their needs and the opportunity for ministry is great (see also 1:35).

6:33 ran on foot. The crowds are now wise to this tactic of simply sailing off across the lake and leaving them standing on the shore (see 4:35-36). So they follow on foot. The distances would not have been great (the lake was only 8 miles at its widest). They could probably see where they were sailing to. As they run around the lake after Jesus, they gathered more and more people.

6:34 a large crowd. It took awhile for Jesus to arrive (perhaps there was no wind that day or a headwind). **sheep without a shepherd**. Without a shepherd, sheep are hopelessly lost. They have no way to defend themselves and they will probably starve. This was an apt metaphor for the condition of the crowd. By and large they had been abandoned by the religious leaders. This phrase is taken from the OT. It is found in Moses' prayer that God send

someone to lead the people of Israel after he dies (Nu 27:17). It is also used in reference to David (Eze 34). This is the first of several allusions to Moses and David.

6:35-36 The disciples recognize that they have a problem on their hands. How are they going to feed the enormous crowd that has gathered? **a remote place**. This is the third reference to a wilderness area (see also vv.31,32). This is another allusion to Moses, who fed the people in the wilderness. Jesus makes this very connection in John 6:26-51. **Send the people away**. This is the disciples' solution! "Let the people buy what they need in the nearby towns." This is not an unreasonable suggestion if the situation is viewed in ordinary terms.

6:37 You give them something to eat. But Jesus has quite a different solution in mind! **eight months of a man's wages**. Once again, as in the storm on the lake (4:37-38), they do not expect Jesus to solve the problem in a miraculous way. The only way they can see to feed the crowd is to buy lots of food. **Are we to go and spend**. This may mean that they did have enough money in their common purse to do this, but were reluctant to spend it this way. Or this may be just a rhetorical question. Their exasperation with Jesus is evident (see 4:38). Mark notes not only Jesus' emotional state (v.34), but also that of the disciples.

6:39 groups on the green grass. A lovely, descriptive touch which could only come from an eyewitness. The people sat in groups in their bright red and yellow robes on the green grass looking like a flower garden spread out across the hills. (The word translated "groups" was used to describe a Greek garden.) It was spring (mid-April), since this was only time the grass was green.

6:40 The division of people into these groups parallels what Moses did (see Ex 18:21).

6:41 five loaves. Small round cakes made of wheat or barley. **two fish**. Probably smoked or pickled fish that was used as a sauce for the bread.

6:42 satisfied. Miraculously, the five loaves and two fish fed everyone not meagerly, but abundantly.

6:43 twelve. The number of the tribes of Israel, reinforcing the idea that what Jesus is doing here has

[Notes continued on page 39]

Mark 6:30-56, continued

Questions

Jesus Walks on the Water

[45]Immediately Jesus made his disciples get into the boat and go on ahead of him to Bethsaida, while he dismissed the crowd. [46]After leaving them, he went up on a mountainside to pray.

[47]When evening came, the boat was in the middle of the lake, and he was alone on land. [48]He saw the disciples straining at the oars, because the wind was against them. About the fourth watch of the night he went out to them, walking on the lake. He was about to pass by them, [49]but when they saw him walking on the lake, they thought he was a ghost. They cried out, [50]because they all saw him and were terrified.

Immediately he spoke to them and said, "Take courage! It is I. Don't be afraid." [51]Then he climbed into the boat with them, and the wind died down. They were completely amazed, [52]for they had not understood about the loaves; their hearts were hardened.

[53]When they had crossed over, they landed at Gennesaret and anchored there. [54]As soon as they got out of the boat, people recognized Jesus. [55]They ran throughout that whole region and carried the sick on mats to wherever they heard he was. [56]And wherever he went—into villages, towns or countryside—they placed the sick in the marketplaces. They begged him to let them touch even the edge of his cloak, and all who touched him were healed.

REFLECT: 1. When was the last time you heard these ill-fated words: "Let's go to a quiet place and get some rest"? What happened instead? How well do you handle such interruptions in your "best laid plans"? **2.** How has Jesus "fed" you when you've been spiritually hungry lately? When you sense that hunger, do you come searching for him, or do you usually try to "fill up" on something else first? Why? **3.** In what area of your life are you "straining at the oars"? How do Jesus' words (v.50) speak to that storm?

Notes, continued

prophetic significance. **basketfuls**. Small wicker containers carried by all Jews. Each disciple returned with his full. **broken pieces**. The law required that the scraps of a meal be collected. **bread**. Bread and eating are recurring themes in these two cycles of stories (6:30-8:26): see 6:31,36-37,42-43; 7:3-4,27-28; 8:1-4,8,14,16,17.

6:44 men. Lit. "males" (see Mt 14:21). When all the women and children are taken into account, this was a huge crowd.

6:45 The reason for Jesus' abrupt dismissal of the disciples and the crowd is explained in the Gospel of John (Jn 6:14-15). Apparently the crowd wanted to make Jesus the king by force. The disciples are sent away, perhaps, to keep them from catching this false Messianic fever. **Bethsaida**. Lit. "house of the fisher." This is a village on the northern shore of the Sea of Galilee several miles east of Capernaum. This was the birthplace of Philip, Andrew, and Peter.

6:46 he went...to pray. In the midst of great success and popular acclaim, once again Jesus goes off to pray. He is quick to acknowledge his dependence on God as the source of his power. Mark recounts three occasions on which Jesus prays on his own. He did so after the initial enthusiastic response to his healing and exorcism in Galilee (1:35); he prays in the Garden of Gethsemane prior to his arrest (14:32-42), and he prays here after the crowds want to proclaim him King. On each occasion, it is dark and Jesus is alone.

6:48 the fourth watch. This was the way Roman soldiers told time. The fourth watch ran from 3:00 to 6:00 a.m. **walking on the lake**. It has already been established that Jesus is Lord over the wind and the water (4:39, 41). This sort of power points to the fact that he is more than just the successor to Moses and David. In the OT, it is God who treads on the water (see Ps 77:19; Job 9:8). **He was about to pass by them**. This could be translated: "for he intended to pass their way," presumably to reveal his presence and remind them of his power in the midst of their distress. Or perhaps Mark's intention is to recall Moses once again and the incident in which God revealed himself to Moses by "passing by" him on Mount Sinai (Ex 33:19-23). This would fit in with previous allusions and amplify the sense that this incident revealed Jesus' divine nature (see v. 50).

6:49 a ghost. The sea, especially at night, was thought to be a dwelling place for demons. Hence the response of the disciples.

6:50 it is I. Lit. "I Am." This phrase can just be a simple declaration by Jesus that he is the "ghost" they are afraid of. However, in the OT this is a phrase used by God to describe himself. (See especially Ex 3:1-14—in the burning bush, God reveals himself by this name to Moses.) This phrase was used by Jesus in his debate with the Jews in which he claims deity (see Jn 8:58). In the context of Jesus' ongoing revelation of himself to the disciples, this is a telling phrase. Jesus is not just a new Moses or the new King in the line of David. He is the Son of God.

6:52 they had not understood about the loaves. The disciples had seen the multiplication of the loaves as just another conjuring trick, rather than understanding what that incident revealed about who Jesus is. They had not understood that he came from God, that he came as the successor to Moses and David, and that he was their true King (i.e., the Messiah). That the feeding of the 5,000 was a crucial event in Jesus' self-revelation is seen in the space Mark devotes to recounting this event (it is, uncharacteristically, longer than that in Matthew or Luke), and by the fact that Mark recounts two feedings, not just one. If the intention was to show Jesus' power, one feeding would suffice. This was an important (though enigmatic) act of self-revelation on the part of Jesus, and Mark wants to make sure his readers get the point, even though the disciples apparently do not. **their hearts were hardened**. This is the problem. Like the Pharisees in the synagogue (3:5—see note), the disciples' hearts are like calcified stone (in Greek the same word is used in both texts). In order for the disciples to recognize who Jesus really is, it will take a miracle to open their hearts to new understanding. In these two cycles of stories, Mark shows Jesus twice performing just such a miracle (7:31-37; 8:22-26), and the response at Caesarea Philippi (8:27-30) demonstrates that he has indeed done this very thing for the disciples. Here in chapter 6, Mark has given three examples of people who misunderstood who Jesus is, and therefore who failed to respond properly to him. The first example is the people in his hometown (6:1-6); the second is Herod (6:14-16); and the third is, surprisingly, the disciples (6:52).

UNIT 12 Clean and Unclean/Syrophoenician Woman/Healing of Deaf and Mute Man

Mark 7:1-37

Clean and Unclean

7 The Pharisees and some of the teachers of the law who had come from Jerusalem gathered around Jesus and ²saw some of his disciples eating food with hands that were "unclean," that is, unwashed. ³(The Pharisees and all the Jews do not eat unless they give their hands a ceremonial washing, holding to the tradition of the elders. ⁴When they come from the marketplace they do not eat unless they wash. And they observe many other traditions, such as the washing of cups, pitchers and kettles. ')

⁵So the Pharisees and teachers of the law asked Jesus, "Why don't your disciples live according to the tradition of the elders instead of eating their food with 'unclean' hands?"

⁶He replied, "Isaiah was right when he prophesied about you hypocrites; as it is written:

" 'These people honor me with their lips,
    but their hearts are far from me.
⁷They worship me in vain;
    their teachings are but rules taught by men.'ᶠ

⁸You have let go of the commands of God and are holding on to the traditions of men."

⁹And he said to them: "You have a fine way of setting aside the commands of God in order to observeᵘ your own traditions! ¹⁰For Moses said, 'Honor your father and your mother,'ᵛ and, 'Anyone who curses his father or mother must be put to death.'ʷ ¹¹But you say that if a man says to his father or mother: 'Whatever help you might otherwise have received from me is Corban' (that is, a gift devoted to God), ¹²then you no longer let him do anything for his father or mother. ¹³Thus you nullify the word of God by your tradition that you have handed down. And you do many things like that."

¹⁴Again Jesus called the crowd to him and said, "Listen to me, everyone, and understand this. ¹⁵Nothing outside a man can make him 'unclean' by going into him. Rather, it is what comes out of a man that makes him 'unclean.'ˣ"

¹⁷After he had left the crowd and entered the house, his disciples asked him about this parable. ¹⁸"Are you so dull?" he asked. "Don't you see that nothing that enters a man from the outside can make him 'unclean'? ¹⁹For it doesn't go into his heart but into his stomach, and then out of his body." (In saying this, Jesus declared all foods "clean.")

Questions

OPEN: 1. In your family, how were you punished for a "foul mouth"? 2. What's the most fun you ever had getting dirty? 3. To what foods did you grow up saying "yecchh!"?

DIG: 1. What is the issue debated by the Pharisees and Jesus? Given this debate, how would each define what it means to be spiritual? How does the quote from Isaiah address the issue at hand? How does the early church continue to help people obey the written law, how is it that they ended up overshadowing that law (vv.8-9)? 3. Something declared "Corban" meant it was dedicated to God, thus it was no longer able to be given away (see notes). What does this illustration show about how traditions twisted the law? 4. How does Jesus' idea of being clean and unclean differ from that of the Pharisees? Why can't external things make an individual unclean? Define each of the polluting acts that Jesus mentions (see notes). 5. Why doesn't Jesus offer any solution to the problem at this time? 6. In verse 24, what is Jesus' point in going to Tyre (a Gentile area) after the discussion in 7:1-23? 7. Were Jesus' words harsh or a play on words? How does this woman take it? How does her reply show faith? 8. What message is Jesus giving by this healing? 9. In verses 31-37, what is significant about where this healing occurred (see 5:1-20)? How does it relate to the debate in 7:1-23? To the prophecy in Isaiah 35:5-6? 10. Why do you think Jesus used this method to heal the man? 11. Why does Jesus now command silence in the Decapolis region (see notes)? 12. How is the response of these Gentiles (v.37) like that of the Jews (1:27; 2:12) and of the Twelve (4:41)? What is Mark's point here?

[Scripture and questions continued on page 42]

ˢ4 Some early manuscripts *pitchers, kettles amd dining couches*   ᶠ6,7 Isaiah 29:13
ᵘ9 some manuscripts *set up*   ᵛ10 Exodus 20:12; Deut. 5:16
ʷ10 Exodus 21:17; Lev. 20:9   ˣ15 Some early manuscripts *'unclean.'*
¹⁶*If anyone has ears to hear, let him hear.*

Notes

7:1-13 It is not just the disciples' hearts that are hard so that the seed of the gospel cannot penetrate; so too are the hearts of the Pharisees, as this story shows.

7:1 *from Jerusalem*. This is the second commission of inquiry sent by a worried religious hierarchy (see 3:22).

7:3-4 Mark explains this ritual washing to his Gentile readers. ***ceremonial washing***. The issue was holiness, not hygiene (germs were unknown in the first century). Before each meal the hands were washed with special water in a particular way. With fingers pointing upward, at least one and one-half eggshells of water was poured over them, and the fist of one hand was rubbed into the fist of the other. Finally, with fingers pointing downward, more water was poured over the hands and allowed to run off at the fingertips. Originally only priests were required to wash in special ways (Ex 30:19). Later, such obligations were extended to all who would be holy. ***the tradition of the elders***. These were the literally thousands of unwritten rules that grew up over time to clarify how the great moral principles of the OT applied in everyday life. A summary of these oral laws was written down in the third century in the Mishnah. ***elders***. Respected Jewish rabbis whose decisions concerning points of religious law were considered authoritative, and therefore binding.

7:6 *Isaiah*. Both Jesus and the Pharisees accept the the authority of the written law (which makes Jesus' use of it here especially powerful). Their dispute is over the unwritten or oral laws which the Pharisees saw as equally binding; a view which Jesus rejects emphatically. ***hypocrites***. This is Mark's only use of this term (though he does refer to hypocrisy in 12:15). In Greek, the word came to mean those who pretend to be something they really are not. Eventually it referred to people who thought they were holy because they kept certain rules and regulations even though their minds, hearts, and actions were actually corrupt.

7:9-13 Jesus illustrates how oral tradition has come to nullify written law. The example he uses has to do with the fifth commandment.

7:11 *Corban*. An oath, which when invoked, dedicated an item to God, rendering it thereafter unavailable for normal use. So, a son might declare his property "Corban" with the result that his parents would have no further claim on his support, even though the oath neither required him to transfer his property to the Temple nor cease using it himself until his death. Such oaths were considered unbreakable.

7:12 The point is that by standing on the traditions of the elders, such a person was able to circumvent the very clear intention of the OT (the written law) that he take care of his parents.

7:13 *nullify the word of God*. This lies at the heart of Jesus' dispute with the Pharisees. They have elevated their traditions over the revealed word of God.

7:14-23 Mark now extends his discussion of what is clean and unclean into a new area: abuse of OT commandments. (The previous section dealt with oral traditions.) The issue is the food laws that so circumscribed first-century Jewish life. Large sections of the OT are devoted to the question of food (e.g., Lev 11; Dt 14:1-21). Jesus' aim is not to attack these laws, but to challenge the assumption that a person was holy before God simply by keeping them. Furthermore, he makes it clear that consuming certain foods does not make a person unfit to participate in fellowship or worship.

7:15 *'unclean'* In Greek, this is a verb that means "to render someone impure in a ritual sense." The idea is that those who come into contact with what is taboo are themselves made unclean, and thus are unfit to worship or to come in contact with others. For the Jew, certain animals were unclean (e.g., pigs and snakes), as were dead bodies, lepers, Gentiles, certain cooking bowls, etc. The OT rules concerning what was clean and unclean were expanded into thousands of specific rules in the oral tradition, many of which were complex and seemingly arbitrary at times.

7:18-19 Jesus has already differed with the Pharisees over eating with outcasts (2:15-17), fasting (2:18-22), and keeping the Sabbath (2:23-28). Here he differs at a fourth point: the effect of ritual defilement. In taking on these ritual laws, Jesus is walking in the steps of certain OT prophets (see Isa 1:10-20; Am 5:21-27) ***heart***. A Jewish idiom for the center of an individual's personality; that which guides that person's thoughts and actions (see also 7:6). ***out of his body***. Lit., "goes into the latrine." ***in saying***

[Notes continued on page 43]   41

Mark 7:1-37, continued

[20]He went on: "What comes out of a man is what makes him 'unclean.' [21]For from within, out of men's hearts, come evil thoughts, sexual immorality, theft, murder, adultery, [22]greed, malice, deceit, lewdness, envy, slander, arrogance and folly. [23]All these evils come from inside and make a man 'unclean.' "

The Faith of a Syrophoenician Woman

[24]Jesus left that place and went to the vicinity of Tyre.[y] He entered a house and did not want anyone to know it; yet he could not keep his presence secret. [25]In fact, as soon as she heard about him, a woman whose little daughter was possessed by an evil[z] spirit came and fell at his feet. [26]The woman was a Greek, born in Syrian Phoenicia. She begged Jesus to drive the demon out of her daughter.

[27]"First let the children eat all they want," he told her, "for it is not right to take the children's bread and toss it to their dogs."

[28]"Yes, Lord," she replied, "but even the dogs under the table eat the children's crumbs."

[29]Then he told her, "For such a reply, you may go; the demon has left your daughter."

[30]She went home and found her child lying on the bed, and the demon gone.

The Healing of a Deaf and Mute Man

[31]Then Jesus left the vicinity of Tyre and went through Sidon, down to the Sea of Galilee and into the region of the Decapolis.[a] [32]There some people brought to him a man who was deaf and could hardly talk, and they begged him to place his hand on the man.

[33]After he took him aside, away from the crowd, Jesus put his fingers into the man's ears. Then he spit and touched the man's tongue. [34]He looked up to heaven and with a deep sigh said to him, *"Ephphatha!"* (which means, "Be opened!"). [35]At this, the man's ears were opened, his tongue was loosened and he began to speak plainly.

[36]Jesus commanded them not to tell anyone. But the more he did so, the more they kept talking about it. [37]People were overwhelmed with amazement. "He has done everything well," they said. "He even makes the deaf hear and the mute speak."

REFLECT: 1. If Jesus came to your community, who are the "unclean" he would care for? How can you be his hands and feet for them? **2.** Jesus walks 100 miles to heal one person. What does that tell you about his willingness to heal? **3.** How has your knowledge of Jesus changed over the past five years? **4.** What can you do this week to show friendship to someone who feels alone because of a certain disability?

[y]24 Many early manuscripts *Tyre and Sidon*   [z]25 Greek *unclean*   [a]31 That is, the Ten Cities

Notes, continued

this Jesus declared all foods "clean." An editorial comment from Mark that was of great significance to his Gentile audience. They are free from OT ceremonial law, he declares. They are not bound by the food (and other) customs of the Jews. As the story of the early church shows, the question of whether Gentiles had to obey Jewish ritual law continued to be a source of debate (see Ac 10; 15:1-29; Ro 14; Gal 2).

7:20-23 It is not whether a person eats kosher food or not that makes him or her pure or impure. The source of impurity is internal (sin within), not external (observance of ritual patterns).

7:21-22 evil thoughts. Evil thoughts precede evil actions. **sexual immorality.** A general term encompassing all acts of sexual impurity. **adultery.** The breach of marriage vows is singled out for mention from the more general term for sexual misconduct. **greed.** The love of having more and more. **malice.** Deliberate wickedness. **deceit.** Cunning. **slander.** Lit. blasphemy. **folly.** Moral and spiritual foolishness.

7:26 a Greek born in Syrian Phoenicia. This woman is described first by her religion, language, and culture. She is a Greek-speaking Gentile. Then she is described by her nationality. She came from Phoenicia (modern-day Lebanon), which was administered by Syria.

7:27 First. Jesus' primary mission is to the children of Israel. However, by the use of the word "first," he implies that a mission to the Gentiles was intended from the beginning. **let the children eat.** The Israelites were often described as the children of God (see Ex 4:22, Hos 11:1) **bread.** Once again food and eating appear in this section (see 6:31, 35-44, 52; 7:2, 5, 19). **dogs.** The reference is to small, household dogs. This is a play on words. On one level, it means simply that the children have the first claim on the food (Jesus' prime ministry is to Israel). On another level, the Jews considered Gentiles "dogs" (using a harsher term which referred to wild street dogs). This woman probably knew this. Jesus echoes this traditional view (which he rejected when he said that nothing is unclean) in an ironic way, using the softened form of the word (lap dogs) and saying it, probably, with a smile on his face.

7:28 She catches on to his word play and replies, in essence, "Carry on with the meal you are serving Israel, but allow us a few scraps."

7:29 for such a reply. Jesus is impressed with the depth of her understanding as well as her clever and witty reply. In fact, this Gentile woman seems to understand more about Jesus than either the Twelve (6:45-56) or the Pharisees (7:1-13)!

7:31-37 Cycle one of this section concludes with the healing of a deaf and dumb man, which seems to have symbolic significance for Mark. It is this sort of miracle of healing that the disciples need if they are to understand properly who Jesus is.

7:32 deaf. Apparently the result of an accident or disease and not a birth defect, since the man could speak some. **could hardly talk.** This is a rare Greek word used only here and in the Greek version of Isaiah 35:5-6. Mark probably intends his readers to understand this healing in the light of the Isaiah passage which proclaims: "Then will the eyes of the blind be opened and the ears of the deaf unstopped. Then will the lame leap like a deer, and the tongue of the dumb shout for joy."

7:33-35 A more complex healing than normal. Perhaps Jesus was using touch to communicate with this deaf man. **spit.** This was regarded by Jews and Greeks as a healing agent. **Ephphatha!** Mark continues to translate for his Roman readers.

7:36 not to tell anyone. This command stands in sharp contrast to what Jesus said on his previous visit to the region of the Decapolis. On that occasion, he told the ex-demoniac *to go and tell* the story of what the Lord had done for him (5:18-20). On this trip, Jesus sees the results of that man's witness. Instead of urgently requesting Jesus to leave as they had done on his previous visit (5:17), now not only do the townspeople bring a man to be healed, but they have developed expectations about who Jesus is and what he can do. Thus Jesus must now command silence, much as he has done regularly in Jewish regions. **they kept talking about it.** Jesus has no better luck getting these Gentiles to be silent than he has had in keeping his healings a secret in Israel (e.g., 1:43-45)!

UNIT 13   Jesus Feeds the Four Thousand/Yeast of Pharisees/Blind Man at Bethsaida

Mark 8:1-26

Jesus Feeds the Four Thousand

8 During those days another large crowd gathered. Since they had nothing to eat, Jesus called his disciples to him and said, [2]"I have compassion for these people; they have already been with me three days and have nothing to eat. [3]If I send them home hungry, they will collapse on the way, because some of them have come a long distance."

[4]His disciples answered, "But where in this remote place can anyone get enough bread to feed them?"

[5]"How many loaves do you have?" Jesus asked.

"Seven," they replied.

[6]He told the crowd to sit down on the ground. When he had taken the seven loaves and given thanks, he broke them and gave them to his disciples to set before the people, and they did so. [7]They had a few small fish as well; he gave thanks for them also and told the disciples to distribute them. [8]The people ate and were satisfied. Afterward the disciples picked up seven basketfuls of broken pieces that were left over. [9]About four thousand men were present. And having sent them away, [10]he got into the boat with his disciples and went to the region of Dalmanutha.

[11]The Pharisees came and began to question Jesus. To test him, they asked him for a sign from heaven. [12]He sighed deeply and said, "Why does this generation ask for a miraculous sign? I tell you the truth, no sign will be given to it." [13]Then he left them, got back into the boat and crossed to the other side.

The Yeast of the Pharisees and Herod

[14]The disciples had forgotten to bring bread, except for one loaf they had with them in the boat. [15]"Be careful," Jesus warned them. "Watch out for the yeast of the Pharisees and that of Herod."

[16]They discussed this with one another and said, "It is because we have no bread."

[17]Aware of their discussion, Jesus asked them: "Why are you talking about having no bread? Do you still not see or understand? Are your hearts hardened? [18]Do you have eyes but fail to see, and ears but fail to hear? And don't you remember? [19]When I broke the five loaves for the five thousand, how many basketfuls of pieces did you pick up?"

"Twelve," they replied.

[20]"And when I broke the seven loaves for the four thousand, how many basketfuls of pieces did you pick up?"

They answered, "Seven."

[21]He said to them, "Do you still not understand?"

Questions

OPEN: 1. How did your parents complete this sentence when you were a child: "How many times have I had to tell you..."? **2.** If you lost your sight, what would you miss seeing the most?

DIG: 1. How does this feeding (vv.1-13) compare and contrast to that of 6:30-44? What is different about the audience (see notes)? **2.** In light of all the miracles that Jesus had already done, why would the Pharisees demand "a sign from heaven"? How might they have responded if Jesus had provided one? **3.** From what you have seen of the Pharisees and Herod so far, what does Jesus mean by his warning in verse 15? How does their "yeast" differ from Jesus' "bread"? How do the disciples take Jesus' comments? What do you find ironic or incredible about this? **4.** With what tone of voice do you hear Jesus saying the words in verses 17-21? What is the main issue here? **5.** How are the numbers "12" and "7" used elsewhere in the Bible? What is Jesus' point in highlighting these numbers? What should the disciples understand about Jesus by these numbers and feedings? How are they like and unlike the Pharisees (vv.11-12)? **6.** Why does Jesus take the man *outside* the city to heal him (v.23)? **7.** What is Jesus' point in healing him in stages, not all at once? **8.** How does this healing compare with the one in 7:31-37? With the disciples' response in 8:17-18? What type of sight do they have?

[Scripture and questions continued on page 46]

Notes

8:1-26 Mark begins a second, parallel cycle of stories (on how the disciples come to recognize Jesus as the Messiah in this unit, see note on 6:30-8:30). If Mark's intention had been simply to recount incidents that reveal Jesus' power, one cycle of stories would have sufficed. But this second cycle alerts the reader to the fact that more is going on here than meets the eye. They must pay attention to what these stories reveal about who Jesus is. These accounts are like parables. On the surface, they say something that is obvious (they are yet more stories about Jesus' power in ministry). But taken together, they add up to something more (they reveal that Jesus is the Messiah). And, like parables, the reader needs to "consider carefully what you hear" (4:24) in order to grasp their meaning.

8:1-10 The major difference between the feeding the 4,000 and the feeding of the 5,000 is the difference in audience. This feeding included Gentiles (as well as Jews), whereas the earlier feeding involved Jews only. The feeding of the 5,000 is about the coming salvation for Israel brought by Jesus, the one who fulfills the mission of Moses and David. The feeding of the 4,000 promises this same salvation to Gentiles.

8:2 *three days*. The crowd had been with him for a few days in contrast to the 5,000, who gathered on the day they were fed (6:33-35).

8:3 *some of them have come a long distance*. This was a phrase used in the Greek OT to describe those who came from Gentile lands (e.g., Isa 60:4, 9; Jer 46:27). By this allusion, Mark hints at the eventual Gentile mission that will gather non-Jews into the church.

8:5 *loaves*. Though fish is once again mentioned (v.7), the emphasis is on bread, both in terms of the feeding stories and in terms of the lessons of these events (6:52; 8:14-21). ***seven***. This is a number often associated with Gentiles.

8:6 *he gave thanks*. This term is used to describe the typical grace that would be said before a meal by Mark's Gentile readers. In contrast, the term used for Jesus' prayer prior to the feeding of the 5,000, though translated "he gave thanks," is literally "he blessed [God]," which is a typical Jewish blessing.

8:10 *Dalmanutha*. It is not certain where this town is located. Possibly it is Magdala, a town near Tiberus on the west side of the lake. The point, however, is clear. At this time Jesus left the Gentile region where he was ministering and returned to Jewish soil.

8:11 *test*. Having just shown who he is by the great miracle of feeding, the Pharisees now want Jesus to prove that he is from God! This is what Jesus has been doing all along, but they are too blind to see it. Jesus refuses their request. Even if he granted it, his sign would probably have been rejected, given the Pharisees' conviction that he was empowered by an evil spirt (see 3:22, 30). They would have condemned him on the basis of Deuteronomy 13:1-5, which warns against following those who do signs and wonders and seek to get people to follow another god. ***a sign from heaven***. What they probably had in mind was something like a vivid display in the sky, or knocking over a house by a word of power. Jesus will not give a sign for its own sake, especially when the request springs from unbelief. His miracles are always in aid of others. Jesus is not just a wonder-worker (see 4:35-6:29).

8:12 *He sighed deeply*. Perhaps in weariness over the seemingly futile disputing with the Pharisees. They just don't get it. This is yet another example of Mark informing the reader about Jesus' emotions (1:41; 3:5; 6:6; 10:14; 14:34).

8:15 *yeast*. To the Jew, yeast was connected with fermentation, which they saw as a form of rotting. So yeast became a metaphor for evil and its expansion. Here it stands for the misunderstanding of the Pharisees, which seems to have spread now even to the disciples (see vv.17-21). It takes only a small amount of yeast to infiltrate a whole batch of bread dough, producing spectacular results. Jesus is not talking about literal yeast (as the disciples took his words to mean— v.16). He is using yeast as a symbol of something else—which is yet another indication of the symbolic nature of this whole unit.

8:16 *They discussed this with one another*. This was probably a quarrel over who forgot the bread. That they should worry about not having enough bread after what had just happened with the 4,000 is incredible.

[Notes continued on page 47]

45

Mark 8:1-26, continued

Questions

The Healing of a Blind Man at Bethsaida

²²They came to Bethsaida, and some people brought a blind man and begged Jesus to touch him. ²³He took the blind man by the hand and led him outside the village. When he had spit on the man's eyes and put his hands on him, Jesus asked, "Do you see anything?"

²⁴He looked up and said, "I see people; they look like trees walking around."

²⁵Once more Jesus put his hands on the man's eyes. Then his eyes were opened, his sight was restored, and he saw everything clearly. ²⁶Jesus sent him home, saying, "Don't go into the village. ᵇ"

REFLECT: 1. Do you sometimes doubt Jesus' ability to meet your needs? How so? How are you discovering that he really can "shepherd" you? In what areas are you still unsure about that? **2.** How can you recognize where the "yeast of the Pharisees and Herod" is still active today? How does it show in the way people relate to God? To one another? **3.** What does "hardness of heart" mean to you? How has Jesus made your heart softer? What part is still hard? **4.** When it comes to understanding Jesus, are you blind? Able to discern blurred shapes? Enjoying 20/20 vision? Explain.

ᵇ26 Some manuscripts *Don't go and tell anyone in the village*

Notes, continued

8:17 *Do you still not see or understand?* Jesus asks this question twice in these verses (vv.14-21). This is the issue. Although exposed to ample evidence of who Jesus is, they still fail to put it all together. *hearts hardened*. This is the problem (see 3:5; 6:52). Their hearts are stone-like. The seed of the word can't penetrate (see 4:15).

8:18 This is actually a quote from Jeremiah 5:21. *eyes but fail to see, and ears but fail to hear?* Now the point of the two healings becomes clear. The disciples are like the deaf man (7:31-35) and the blind man (8:22-25). They too need a miracle from Jesus in order to see and hear properly. That such a miracle takes place becomes evident in the final story in this unit: the confession at Caesarea Philippi that Jesus is the Messiah (8:27-29).

8:19-21 A notoriously difficult passage to interpret. *how many*. Jesus' repetition of this question points to the fact that the numbers are important in understanding the meaning of the feedings. They reveal him to be the long-expected Messiah who brings salvation to Israel and to the whole world. *Twelve*. A symbol standing for Israel. *Seven*. A symbol standing for the Gentile nations.

8:22-26 There are clear parallels between this healing and the healing of the deaf and dumb man in 7:31-37. The healing of this blind man is unusual in that it requires two touches on the part of Jesus. As with so much else in this unit, this healing symbolizes something else. Specifically, the "blind" disciples (vv.17-18) are about to receive their "first touch" of healing. In the next story, Peter will declare that they know that Jesus is the Messiah (8:27-30). This is a great step forward in their understanding. However, they have not fully understood who Jesus is, as Peter's vigorous rejection of Jesus' teaching about the Messiah demonstrates (8:31-33). They need a second touch to open their eyes completely. This will not come until Jesus dies and rises again.

8:24 *they look like trees*. He probably once had his sight, since he knows what a tree looks like.

UNIT 14 Peter's Confession/Jesus Predicts His Death

Mark 8:27-9:1

Peter's Confession of Christ

²⁷Jesus and his disciples went on to the villages around Caesarea Philippi. On the way he asked them, "Who do people say I am?"

²⁸They replied, "Some say John the Baptist; others say Elijah; and still others, one of the prophets."

²⁹"But what about you?" he asked. "Who do you say I am?" Peter answered, "You are the Christ.ᶜ"

³⁰Jesus warned them not to tell anyone about him.

Jesus Predicts His Death

³¹He then began to teach them that the Son of Man must suffer many things and be rejected by the elders, chief priests and teachers of the law, and that he must be killed and after three days rise again. ³²He spoke plainly about this, and Peter took him aside and began to rebuke him.

³³But when Jesus turned and looked at his disciples, he rebuked Peter. "Get behind me, Satan!" he said. "You do not have in mind the things of God, but the things of men."

³⁴Then he called the crowd to him along with his disciples and said: "If anyone would come after me, he must deny himself and take up his cross and follow me. ³⁵For whoever wants to save his lifeᵈ will lose it, but whoever loses his life for me and for the gospel will save it. ³⁶What good is it for a man to gain the whole world, yet forfeit his soul? ³⁷Or what can a man give in exchange for his soul? ³⁸If anyone is ashamed of me and my words in this adulterous and sinful generation, the Son of Man will be ashamed of him when he comes in his Father's glory with the holy angels."

9 And he said to them, "I tell you the truth, some who are standing here will not taste death before they see the kingdom of God come with power."

Questions

OPEN: 1. What word most often describes you? **2.** If you could live anywhere in the world, where would you choose? Why?

DIG: 1. Thus far, what answers have been given to Jesus' question in verse 27 (3:21,22; 4:41; 5:17; 6:3,14-15)? What do you make of these answers? **2.** How and why does the tone of the gospel shift after Peter's declaration? **3.** What title does Jesus take on, and why (see Da 7:13-14)? What four things does he prophesy about the Son of Man? According to Jesus, what kind of Messiah is he? Why does Jesus react so strongly to Peter? What does Peter have in common with Satan (see Mt 4:8-10)? **4.** How is Peter like the blind beggar (8:22-26)? How does this explain why Jesus told them not to tell anyone about him (v.30)? **5.** How would you paraphrase what Jesus says in verse 34? How have Herod and John (6:14-29) illustrated the principle of verses 35-36? What does it really mean to believe in Jesus?

REFLECT: 1. Recently, how has your relationship with Jesus affected your lifestyle? Relationships? Priorities? Politics? **2.** In what area does "Jesus' way" conflict with "your way" now? How is the gospel of *self-denial* different than the gospel of *self-fulfillment*? What is the cost-benefit ratio of each course of action?

ᶜ29 Or *Messiah*. "The Christ" (Greek) and "the Messiah" (Hebrew) both mean "the Anointed One." ᵈ35 The Greek word means either *life* or *soul*; also in verse 36.

TIME
FOR A
CHECK-UP

SEVEN COMMON SMALL GROUP AILMENTS
AND HOW TO OVERCOME THEM

ARE YOU FEELING A LITTLE
NERVOUS ABOUT BEING IN A SMALL GROUP?

SYMPTOMS: Do you break out into a sweat at the mention of small groups. Does your mouth turn to sawdust when it comes "your turn" to share? To pray?

PRESCRIPTION: Take this test to see if you are ready to belong to a small group. If you answer "yes" on seven out of ten questions below, you are probably ready to take the plunge.

1. Are you looking for a place where you can deal with the serious questions in your life right now?   ☐ Yes   ☐ No

2. Are you open to the possibility that God has something special for your life?
   ☐ Yes   ☐ No

3. Are you open to the Bible as the source where God's will for your life can be explored?
   ☐ Yes   ☐ No

4. Are you able to admit that you do not have all the answers about the Bible? God? Your own life?   ☐ Yes   ☐ No

5. Are you able to let others have questions about the Bible or God?   ☐ Yes   ☐ No

6. Are you willing to accept people in the group that are "Prodigal Sons" and have a long way to go in their spiritual faith?   ☐ Yes   ☐ No

7. Are you willing to keep anything that is shared in this group in strict confidence?   ☐ Yes   ☐ No

8. Are you willing to share in the responsibility for the group and to support group members with your prayers?   ☐ Yes   ☐ No

9. Are you willing to give priority to this group for a short period of time (such as six to twelve weeks) and consider making a longer commitment after this time?
   ☐ Yes   ☐ No

10. Are you excited about the possibilities of belonging to a group that could make a difference in your life?   ☐ Yes   ☐ No

ARE YOU FEELING A LITTLE
CONFUSED ABOUT YOUR PURPOSE?

SYMPTOMS: Do you feel like you are playing on a team that doesn't have any rules? Any direction? Any idea of what you want to do or accomplish? Or where you are going?

PRESCRIPTION: Before you ever started the group, you should have decided on a COVENANT that spelled out your purpose, rules, expectations, etc. If you didn't, call "time out" and decide *together* on a covenant.

Here's how. Take the first sentence below and ask everyone to finish the sentence. Then, try to come up with a one sentence statement that you all can agree to. "The purpose of our group is . . ."

Then, take the second sentence and decide on your specific goals, etc. . . . until you have decided on your GROUP COVENANT. This becomes your game plan.

1. The purpose of our group is . . .

2. Our specific goals are . . .

3. We will meet _____ times, every _____ week, after which we will evaluate our group.

4. We will meet: Day of week _____ from _____ (time) to _____ .

5. We will meet at _____ , or rotate the place where we meet.

6. In addition to the study of the Bible, we will . . .

7. We will adhere to the following ground rules:
   □ The leader of the group will be . . . or we will rotate the leadership.
   □ The host for each meeting (other than the leader) will be . . . or we will rotate this responsibility.
   □ Food/refreshments will be . . .
   □ Baby-sitting, etc.

8. In addition to these general rules, we will agree to the following disciplines:
   □ Attendance: To give priority to the group meetings
   □ Participation: To share responsibility for the group
   □ Confidentiality: To keep anything that is said strictly confidential
   □ Accountability: To give permission to group members to hold you accountable for goals you set for yourself
   □ Accessibility: To give one another the right to call upon you for help in time of need—even in the middle of the night.

ARE YOU FEELING A LITTLE

DISTANT FROM THE OTHERS IN YOUR GROUP?

SYMPTOMS: Does your group start off like a Model A Ford on a cold morning? Or sag in the middle when you get to the Bible study? Do you find some of the people do all the talking . . . and others never get out of their "shell"?

PRESCRIPTION: Use the "flow questions" in the margin, next to the Scripture text, to guide the discussion. The questions are carefully designed to explode like time bombs on three levels of sharing: (1) OPEN—to break the ice, (2) DIG—to discuss the Scripture text, and (3) REFLECT—to take inventory of your own life.

OPEN/10-15 Minutes: ⟶
Start off with a few good "stories" about your childhood or human-interest experiences. The better the "stories" at this level . . . the deeper the group will share at the close. (There is a close parallel between "childlikeness" and "Christlikeness".

> OPEN: 1. When you were growing up, who were the people you were told not to associate with? What part of the city or country would you be warned about? What would have happened if you had gone there? 2. Where was the "watering hole" in your home town, where everybody went to "hang out"?

DIG/30-45 Minutes: ⟶
You read the Scripture text at this point and go around on the first question . . . looking to the text for your answers. The questions are designed to force the group into observation/interpretation. (This is called the "inductive method" to Bible study). By the way, you do not have to finish all the questions. Save time at the close for Reflect.

> DIG: 1. From 1:19-28 and 3:22-26, why might Jesus decide to "get out of town" in a hurry? 2. As someone taught from birth to despise the Samaritans, how would you feel when Jesus decided to go through Samaria instead of the long way home? 3. Since "nice" girls did not come to the water well at, noontime ("the sixth hour"), why do think Jesus risked his reputation to ask a favor of this woman? 4. How would

REFLECT/15-30 Minutes: ⟶
This is the heart of the Bible study. The purpose is to take inventory of your own life and share with the group "what God is telling you to do." The questions are "high risk"; that is, the group is asked to share on a "need level", before moving on to prayer.

> REFLECT: 1. What social, ethnic, or religious barriers are difficult for you to break through? How would Jesus relate to these people you find difficult? 2. What aspects of Jesus' conversation could you use as a model for your own discussions with searching friends?

FLOW QUESTIONS/DISCLOSURE SCALE

At the beginning of the meeting: Ice breaker questions.	In the middle of the meeting: Bible search questions.	At the close of the meeting: Personal inventory.
LOW RISK	MODERATE RISK	HIGH RISK

Philippians 1:3-11

Thanksgiving and Prayer

³I thank my God every time I remember you. ⁴In all my prayers for all of you, I always pray with joy ⁵because of your partnership in the gospel from the first day until now, ⁶being confident of this, that he who began a good work in you will carry it on to completion until the day of Christ Jesus.

⁷It is right for me to feel this way about all of you, since I have you in my heart; for whether I am in chains or defending and confirming the gospel, all of you share in God's grace with me. ⁸God can testify how I long for all of you with the affection of Christ Jesus.

⁹And this is my prayer: that your love may abound more and more in knowledge and depth of insight, ¹⁰so that you may be

Questions

OPEN: When you care for someone, are you more likely to send a funny card or a touching one? What card still brings back a smile (or a warm fuzzy) for you?

DIG: 1. What are Paul's feelings for this church? What does that show about his leadership style? **2.** What is the "good work" to be completed (v.6)? How so (see 2:12-13)? **3.** What qualities are key to a fellowship (vv.9-11)?

REFLECT: What concerns for your group does Paul's prayer bring to mind? Paraphrase and personalize Paul's prayer to make it your own.

ARE YOU FEELING A LITTLE
INTIMIDATED BY THE BIBLE SCHOLARS IN YOUR GROUP?

SYMPTOMS: Are you afraid that your ignorance about the Bible could be embarrassing? For instance: if someone asked you who Melchizedek was, what would you say? If you said "an old linebacker for the Raiders", you would be wrong. Twice wrong.

PRESCRIPTION: Don't despair. Most of the people in your group don't know either. And that's O.K. This Bible study group is for BEGINNERS. And for BEGINNERS, there are Notes on the opposite page to help you keep up to speed with the rest of the group.

NOTES include:

☐ Definitions of significant words.

☐ Historical background: the political, social, economic context behind the words in the text.

☐ Geographical setting: facts about the country, terrain, lakes, crops, roads, and religious shrines.

☐ Cultural perspective: lifestyles, homes, customs, holidays, traditions, and social patterns.

☐ Archeological evidence: recent findings that sheds light on the Bible events.

☐ Summary/Commentary: recap of the argument to keep the passage in the context of the whole book.

Notes

1:3 every time I remember you. This is a difficult phrase to translate from the Greek. What it seems to mean is that during his times of prayer, Paul "was compelled by love to mention his Philippian friends. This means, then, that Paul gave thanks not whenever he happened to remember them, but that he regularly gave thanks for them and mentioned them to God at set times of prayer" (Hawthorne).

1:4 with joy. "Joy" is a theme that pervades Philippians. This is the first of some fourteen times that Paul will use the word in this epistle. He mentions "joy" more often in this short epistle

confirming the gospel. These are legal terms. The reference is to Paul's defense before the Roman court, in which he hopes to be able not only to vindicate himself and the gospel from false charges, but to proclaim the gospel in life-changing power to those in the courtroom. (See Ac 26 for an example of how Paul did this when he stood in court before Agrippa and Festus.)

1:8 I long. Yet another word characteristic of Paul. He uses it seven of the nine times it is found in the New Testament. This is a strong word and expresses the depth of Paul's feelings for them, his desire to be with them, and the wish to minister

ARE YOU FEELING A LITTLE

TEMPTED TO KEEP THE GROUP JUST FOR YOURSELF?

SYMPTOMS: Two feelings surface: (1) if we let anyone into our group, it would destroy our "closeness", and/or (2) if we let anyone into our group, we would not have time enough to share.

PRESCRIPTION: Study the ministry of Jesus and the early church: the need for "closeness" and the danger of "closedness." How did Jesus respond to his own disciples when they asked to "stay together" and build a "monument." Note the Story of the Transfiguration in Mark 9:2–13.

SOLUTION #1: Pull up an empty chair during the prayer time at the close of the group and pray that God will "fill the chair" with someone by the next week.

SOLUTION #2: When the group reaches seven or eight in number, divide into two groups of 4—4 at the dining table, 4 at the kitchen table—when the time comes for the Bible study . . . and reshuffle the foursomes every week so that you keep the whole group intact, but sub-group for the discussion time.

THREE PART AGENDA FOR GROUP USING THE SUB-GROUP MODEL

GATHERING/15 Minutes/All Together.
Refreshments are served as the group gathers and assignments are made to sub-groups of 4.

SHARING/30–45 Minutes/Groups of 4.
Sub-groups are formed to discuss the questions in the margin of the text.

CARING/15–30 Minutes/All Together.
Regather the whole group to share prayer requests and pray.

ARE YOU FEELING A LITTLE
BORED WITH YOUR BIBLE STUDY GROUP?

SYMPTOMS: You feel "tired" before the meeting starts. And worse after it is over. The sharing is mostly a "head-trip". One person is absent three weeks in a row. Another is chronically late. You feel like your time could be better spent doing something else, but you don't know how to say it.

PRESCRIPTION: You may be having a group "mid-life" crisis. Here are three suggestions.

1. Call "time out" for a session and evaluate your Covenant (page 5). Are you focused on your "purpose"? Your goals? Are you sticking to your rules? Should you throw out some of your rules? (Nobody said you can't.)

2. Check to see if your group is hitting on all three cylinders for a healthy small group. (1) Nurture/Bible Study, (2) Support for one another, and (3) Mission/Task. Here's a way to test yourself.
   On a scale from 1 to 10, circle a number to indicate how you feel your group is doing on each of these three cylinders.

   ON NURTURE/BIBLE STUDY: Getting to know the Bible. Letting God speak to you about His plans for your life through the Scripture.

We're doing a LOUSY JOB	1	2	3	4	5	6	7	8	9	10	We're doing a GREAT JOB

   ON SUPPORT: Getting to know each other. Caring about each other. Holding each other accountable for the best God has for you.

We're doing a LOUSY JOB	1	2	3	4	5	6	7	8	9	10	We're doing a GREAT JOB

   ON MISSION/TASK: Reaching out to others in need. Drawing people into the group, or sponsoring another group.

We're doing a LOUSY JOB	1	2	3	4	5	6	7	8	9	10	We're doing a GREAT JOB

3. Consider the possibility that God is saying it is time to shut down the group. Take time for a party. Give everyone a chance to share what the group has meant to him/her and what he/she will remember most about the group.

ARE YOU FEELING A LITTLE

ITCHY ABOUT DOING SOMETHING MORE?

SYMPTOMS: You're feeling tired of just sitting around studying the Bible. You have friends who are really hurting. Struggling. God seems to be saying something, but you don't know just what.

PRESCRIPTION: Consider the possibility that God is asking your group to split up and give birth to some new groups. Here are some steps:

1. Brainstorm together. Go around and have everyone finish the first sentence below. Then, go around on the second sentence, etc.

   I am concerned about a group for . . . (such as . . . "a group for young mothers, single parents, blended families, parents of adolescents, men at my office, young couples, empty nesters . . ." etc.).

   I wish we could . . .

   I would be willing to . . .

2. Make a list of prospects (people from the fringe of the church or outside of any church) that you would like to invite to a dinner party at which you could explain "what this Bible study group has meant to you."

3. Write each of these people a hand-written invitation on your personal stationary, inviting them to the dinner party at your home. (Don't bother to use the church bulletin. Nobody reads that.)

HOW TO TURN YOUR GROUP INTO A MISSIONARY GROUP

ORIGINAL
STUDY
GROUP

Holds a dinner party
for their friends
and prospects

NEW STUDY GROUPS ARE FORMED/ORIGINAL GROUP THE LEADERS

(P.S. You can still get back together with the whole group once a month for a "reunion" to share exciting "stories" of your new groups.

Notes

8:27-30 This is a pivotal passage in the Gospel of Mark. The disciples declare (through Peter, who seems to have become their spokesman) that they recognize who Jesus is. He is the long-expected Messiah. To be sure, they have the wrong idea about the nature and role of the Messiah. But at least they have grasped accurately that Jesus is not just an exceptional rabbi, nor just a wonder-worker.

8:27 *Caesarea Philippi*. A beautiful city on the slopes of Mt. Hermon, 25 miles north of Bethsaida. This region reeked with religion. It had been a center of Baal worship, and was said to be the birthplace of the god Pan. It was also the place where the River Jordan began. At the time when Jesus and his disciples visited there, up on the hill was a gleaming, white marble temple dedicated to the godhead of Caesar. It is fitting that in this place with rich associations to the religions of the world, Jesus, the Galilean, asks his disciples if they understand that he is the Anointed One sent by God. **Who do you say I am?** This is *the* question. Do the disciples yet see? Have they grasped the meaning of Jesus?

8:29 *You are the Christ*. Peter identifies him as the Messiah. "Christ" is the Greek term for "Messiah" (which is a Hebrew word). Both terms mean "the Anointed One," the prophesied king of Israel.

8:30 Jesus urges them to be silent about what they know. The problem is that although they know that he is the Messiah, they do not yet know what kind of Messiah he is—as the next incident shows (8:31-33).

8:31-10:52 This is the start of the fourth major unit in the Gospel of Mark, which focuses on Jesus in his role as teacher. This unit is organized around Jesus' three predictions that he will die and rise again (8:31; 9:31; 10:32-34; see also 9:9-13). In each case, the disciples fail to grasp what Jesus is saying (see 8:32-33; 9:32-37; 10:35-45). It is not until they receive a "second touch" that they are able to see clearly. Fittingly, the unit ends with the healing of blind Bartimaeus. The final week of Jesus' life begins then. It is as a result of his death and resurrection that the Twelve finally grasp that he is not just the Messiah, but that he is also the Son of God. This is the second touch they need. This unit also contains Jesus' teaching on discipleship (see 8:34-38: 9:33-50; 10:13-31, 35-45).

8:31 This is the first of the three predictions. To predict one's death is rare, but not unknown. How-ever, to predict that one will then rise from the dead is startling. No wonder the disciples had trouble taking in what he was saying. The repetition three times of this prediction of death and resurrection draws attention to its central importance in understanding who Jesus is. ***rejected by the elders, chief priests and teachers of the law***. These three groups made up the Sanhedrin, the ruling Jewish body. Jesus is predicting that he will be officially rejected by Israel (see 14:55). **He then began to teach them**. For the remainder of this unit (8:31-10:52), Jesus seeks to teach the Twelve what kind of Messiah he is. **Son of Man**. This is the title that Jesus prefers for himself. In the first century it was a rather colorless, indeterminate title (with some messianic overtones) which could be translated as "man" or even "I." This allows Jesus to fill it with new meaning and to convey what kind of Messiah he actually is.

8:32 *rebuke*. Peter, who moments before identifies Jesus as the Messiah, is startled by his teaching that the Messiah will suffer, be rejected, killed, and then rise from the dead. He felt compelled to take Jesus aside and urge him to stop this line of teaching. The word "rebuke" is the same one used to describe the silencing of demons.

8:33 *Out of my sight, Satan!* By urging Jesus to back away from his teaching about suffering and death, Peter is doing what Satan did: tempting Jesus with the promise that he can have the whole world without pain (Mt 4:8-10).

8:34-38 Jesus defines what following him means. It involves denial, cross-bearing, and losing one's life. The original recipients of the letter (the Christians in Rome) were doing this very thing: suffering for the sake of Jesus. **the crowd**. In all likelihood, this was not what the crowd wanted to hear. It was not self-denial that drew them to Jesus, but self-fulfillment (healing, exorcism, teaching). **cross**. This word is used prior to Jesus' death on a cross. It would evoke for his hearers the image of Roman execution—to be a follower of Jesus might involve execution by the state. **save his life**. The image is of a trial in which one is called upon to renounce Jesus in order to live.

9:1 Jesus announces that a momentous event (which will demonstrate that the kingdom of God has indeed come) will soon take place. Six days later the transfiguration occurs (9:2-8).

UNIT 15 Transfiguration/Healing of a Boy with an Evil Spirit

Mark 9:2-32

The Transfiguration

²After six days Jesus took Peter, James and John with him and led them up a high mountain, where they were all alone. There he was transfigured before them. ³His clothes became dazzling white, whiter than anyone in the world could bleach them. ⁴And there appeared before them Elijah and Moses, who were talking with Jesus.

⁵Peter said to Jesus, "Rabbi, it is good for us to be here. Let us put up three shelters—one for you, one for Moses and one for Elijah." ⁶(He did not know what to say, they were so frightened.)

⁷Then a cloud appeared and enveloped them, and a voice came from the cloud: "This is my Son, whom I love. Listen to him!"

⁸Suddenly, when they looked around, they no longer saw anyone with them except Jesus.

⁹As they were coming down the mountain, Jesus gave them orders not to tell anyone what they had seen until the Son of Man had risen from the dead. ¹⁰They kept the matter to themselves, discussing what "rising from the dead" meant.

¹¹And they asked him, "Why do the teachers of the law say that Elijah must come first?"

¹²Jesus replied, "To be sure, Elijah does come first, and restores all things. Why then is it written that the Son of Man must suffer much and be rejected? ¹³But I tell you, Elijah has come, and they have done to him everything they wished, just as it is written about him."

The Healing of a Boy With an Evil Spirit

¹⁴When they came to the other disciples, they saw a large crowd around them and the teachers of the law arguing with them. ¹⁵As soon as all the people saw Jesus, they were overwhelmed with wonder and ran to greet him.

¹⁶"What are you arguing with them about?" he asked.

¹⁷A man in the crowd answered, "Teacher, I brought you my son, who is possessed by a spirit that has robbed him of speech. ¹⁸Whenever it seizes him, it throws him to the ground. He foams at the mouth, gnashes his teeth and becomes rigid. I asked your disciples to drive out the spirit, but they could not."

¹⁹"O unbelieving generation," Jesus replied, "how long shall I stay with you? How long shall I put up with you? Bring the boy to me."

Questions

OPEN: Of all the places called "God's country," which one is your favorite?

DIG: 1. What is the connection between 9:1 and this event? What other divine revelations are associated with "six days," "high mountain," and "dazzling white" (see notes)? **2.** What do you imagine this scene was like? What is the significance of Moses' and Elijah's presence? Of the voice and cloud (v.7; see 1:11; Dt 18:15)? Why would this be important for Jesus at this stage of his ministry? Why would it be important for the disciples? **3.** Why did Jesus take the three if he didn't want them to tell anyone what happened (see also 5:37-41; 8:32)? **4.** Who played the role of Elijah (see Mt 17:10-13)? With what result (6:14-29)? How could John the Baptist's experience help the disciples understand the nature of Jesus' Messiahship? **5.** While the three disciples were up on the mountain (v.14), what problem were the other nine having? How did they deal with it? How might verses 2-3 account for the "wonder" with which the others greeted Jesus? What do you think the argument was about in verse 14? **6.** As the boy's father, how would you feel during this argument? How could the father doubt and believe at the same time? **7.** How do the contrasts between this story and the transfiguration account for Jesus' response in verse 19? What stories from Mark further illustrate Jesus' point about the unbelieving generation? **8.** What is the major difference between Jesus' teaching in 8:31 and in 9:30-32? What is significant about this difference? **9.** What does this story teach about faith in relation to unbelief? In relation to prayer?

[Scripture and questions continued on page 52]

Notes

9:2-13 The account of the transfiguration parallels in some interesting ways the baptism of Jesus (1:9-11). In the same way that the baptism of Jesus opened the first half of the Gospel (after some preliminary words from the OT and from John the Baptist), the transfiguration opens the second half (following some defining words by Jesus). In both incidents, the voice of God affirms that Jesus is his special Son. Both draw heavily on the OT for their meaning. The baptism of Jesus prefigures his death; the transfiguration, his resurrection.

9:2 *After six days*. By this phrase Mark connects the transfiguration with Jesus' prediction that "some who are standing here will not taste death before they see the kingdom of God come with power" (9:1). The mention of "six days" is probably also an allusion to Exodus 25:15-18, where the story is told of Moses going up the mountain and remaining there six days until he is summoned into the presence of God. Thus the readers are alerted to the fact that another revelation of God is about to take place. ***Peter, James and John***. These three emerge as an inner circle around Jesus. Mark has pointed out that Jesus took only these three disciples with him when he raised Jairus' daughter (5:37-41). Here he selects them to accompany him up the mountain. These are three of the first four disciples Jesus chose (1:14-20). ***a high mountain***. This may well be Mt. Hermon, a 9,000 foot mountain located some twelve miles from Caesarea Philippi (though early tradition says it is Mt. Tabor, located southwest of the Sea of Galilee). It was on other mountains in times past that God revealed himself: for example, to Moses on Mt. Sinai (Ex 24) and to Elijah on Mt. Horeb (1Ki 19). ***transfigured***. The word used here is *metamorphothe* (from which the English word "metamorphosis" comes). It means, lit., "to change one's form."

9:3 *dazzling white*. The word "dazzling" (or "radiant") was used to describe the glistening of highly-polished metal or the sparkling of sunlight. The phrase "dazzling white" is also found in Da 7:9, where it is used to describe the clothing of God when he appeared in a vision. Here the disciples witness Jesus being changed into a form just like God. In Revelation 1:9-18, the resurrected, glorified Jesus is described with this same term.

9:4 *Elijah*. Elijah was a great prophet. The Jews expected that he would return just prior to the coming of the salvation they had been promised. And indeed, he is there on the mountain as the forerunner of the Messiah. ***Moses***. Moses was the greatest figure in the OT. It was to him God gave the law which became the very heart of the nation. It was he who brought the religion of Israel into being. And it was Moses who prophesied that God would one day send another prophet to lead his people (Dt 18:15). The early Christians took this to be a prophecy about Jesus (Ac 3:22-26; 7:35-37). Both Moses and Elijah endorse Jesus and testify to his greatness.

9:5 *shelters*. Peter might have had in mind the huts of intertwined branches which were put up at the Festival of Tabernacles to commemorate Israel's time in the wilderness. Or he might be thinking of the "tent of meeting" where God met with Moses. In making this suggestion, Peter shows his (quite understandable) confusion about this event. Did it mark the full arrival of the kingdom? Did this mean that Jesus had come into his glory without the suffering he told them about? How should he respond to such an amazing experience?

9:7 *a voice*. Once again, as he did at the baptism of Jesus (1:11), God proclaims that Jesus is his Son. ***the cloud***. In the OT when God appeared, it was often in a cloud (Ex 16:10; 19:9; 24:15-18; 40:34-38). ***This is my Son***. By means of this event, it is revealed that not only is Jesus the Messiah (as the disciples have just confessed), he is also the Son of God. Both titles are necessary for a full understanding of his nature and role. The second half of the Gospel is about the discovery that Jesus is the Son of God. ***Listen to him!*** This is a quotation from Moses' prophecy about the coming prophet (see note for 9:4).

9:9-11 The disciples discuss the Jewish expectation that Elijah will come to inaugurate the kingdom. They do not really grasp the significance of the transfiguration (nor the need for suffering and death on the part of the Messiah), nor can they until after Jesus' resurrection. Their two questions spring from confusion over Jesus' radically new teaching (about suffering, death and resurrection) in light of popular expectations about the Messiah.

[Notes continued on page 53]   51

Mark 9:2-32, continued

[20]So they brought him. When the spirit saw Jesus, it immediately threw the boy into a convulsion. He fell to the ground and rolled around, foaming at the mouth.

[21]Jesus asked the boy's father, "How long has he been like this?"

"From childhood," he answered. [22]"It has often thrown him into fire or water to kill him. But if you can do anything, take pity on us and help us."

[23]" 'If you can'?" said Jesus. "Everything is possible for him who believes."

[24]Immediately the boy's father exclaimed, "I do believe; help me overcome my unbelief!"

[25]When Jesus saw that a crowd was running to the scene, he rebuked the evil[ꞌ] spirit. "You deaf and mute spirit," he said, "I command you, come out of him and never enter him again."

[26]The spirit shrieked, convulsed him violently and came out. The boy looked so much like a corpse that many said, "He's dead." [27]But Jesus took him by the hand and lifted him to his feet, and he stood up.

[28]After Jesus had gone indoors, his disciples asked him privately, "Why couldn't we drive it out?"

[29]He replied, "This kind can come out only by prayer.[ꞌ]"

[30]They left that place and passed through Galilee. Jesus did not want anyone to know where they were, [31]because he was teaching his disciples. He said to them, "The Son of Man is going to be betrayed into the hands of men. They will kill him, and after three days he will rise." [32]But they did not understand what he meant and were afraid to ask him about it.

REFLECT: 1. What spot for you is most like the Mount of Transfiguration—where you grasped a bit of Jesus' glory in a special way? **2.** How does the picture of a suffering Messiah shape your view of what the Christian life is all about? **3.** When have you felt like the father in verse 24? How do prayer and faith relate for you at those times? **4.** Where do you learn more—highs or lows? Why isn't the Christian life more like a plateau experience? **5.** How can you live with the full reality of evil and yet with strong awareness of God's transforming power? In what way do you feel that tension now? **6.** What possibilities and what abuses come to mind when you ponder the fact that "everything is possible for him who believes" (v.23)?

[ꞌ]25 Greek *unclean*   [ꞌ]29 Some manuscripts *prayer and fasting*

Notes, continued

9:12 _it is written_. Jesus does not specify which OT passage he has in mind, though a passage like Isaiah 53:3 would explain his statement here and in 8:31 that the Son of Man "must suffer" and die.

9:13 _Elijah has come_. Here, in the transfiguration, the long-expected Elijah comes. However, Elijah has come in a second sense. John the Baptist has played the role of Elijah by being the forerunner of the Messiah.

9:14-32 Jesus and his three disciples descend from the "high" of this mountaintop experience to the valley, where the other disciples are arguing with the religious leaders about their failure to cast out a demon. They go from the experience of God's power and presence to the experience of Satan's power and presence. The movement from transfiguration to confrontation with evil parallels the earlier movement of Jesus from baptism to the wilderness of temptation. This also parallels Moses' experience when he returned down from the mountain to find the people of Israel worshiping a golden calf (Ex 32). This is the final exorcism in the Gospel of Mark.

9:18 The symptoms closely resemble those of a certain form of epilepsy. **_they could not_**. The faith of the disciples is shown once again to be incomplete.

9:19 _O unbelieving generation_. This is the cry of anguish and loneliness of one who knows so clearly the way things really are, and yet is constantly confronted with disbelief in various forms. **_how long shall I stay with you?_** The time will come when the disciples are on their own to carry on the work of the kingdom.

9:23 _'If you can'?_ By this phrase, the man indicates that he is not sure if Jesus can perform such a miracle (after all, his disciples have failed).

By highlighting his doubts Jesus pinpoints the real issue: the question is not whether Jesus has the ability to heal (which has been amply demonstrated); the issue is the man's ability to believe.

9:24 _believe_. Belief or "faith is the assertion of a possibility against all probabilities, in spite of any contrary indications provided by our experience of life or of the realities of the world....What is it that differentiates this faith from mere illusion...? It is not a faith which reaches vaguely into the void, but one that firmly trusts a Jesus Christ" (Lane). **_unbelief_**. The problem here is one of _doubt_ (being in two minds about an issue) not one of _disbelief_ (certainty that something is not true). The father did not disbelieve. After all, he had brought his son to Jesus to be healed (v. 17). His faith has been shaken, however, by the failure of the disciples to heal his son (v.18) so that now, even though he desperately wants his child to be free of this demon, he wonders if it is possible (v.22).

9:29 _prayer_. The disciples have been given the authority to cast out demons (6:7) and have, in fact, done so (6:13). However, as this incident makes clear, this power was not their own. It required continuing dependence upon God.

9:31 For the second time, Jesus warns them of what lies ahead. **_betrayed_**. This is a new note in his teaching. It is not just that he will be rejected by the leaders of Israel. There will be an element of treachery involved. This same word is used again by Mark in 14:41-42 to describe Judas' betrayal of Jesus.

9:32 Once again they fail to grasp what Jesus is saying. His talk of betrayal, death, and resurrection is so far from their understanding of what the Messiah would be like that they simply cannot take in his words.

UNIT 16 Who is Greatest/Whoever Is Not Against Us/Causing to Sin/Divorce

Mark 9:33-10:12

Who Is the Greatest?

³³They came to Capernaum. When he was in the house, he asked them, "What were you arguing about on the road?" ³⁴But they kept quiet because on the way they had argued about who was the greatest.

³⁵Sitting down, Jesus called the Twelve and said, "If anyone wants to be first, he must be the very last, and the servant of all."

³⁶He took a little child and had him stand among them. Taking him in his arms, he said to them, ³⁷"Whoever welcomes one of these little children in my name welcomes me; and whoever welcomes me does not welcome me but the one who sent me."

Whoever Is Not Against Us Is for Us

³⁸"Teacher," said John, "we saw a man driving out demons in your name and we told him to stop, because he was not one of us."

³⁹"Do not stop him," Jesus said. "No one who does a miracle in my name can in the next moment say anything bad about me, ⁴⁰for whoever is not against us is for us. ⁴¹I tell you the truth, anyone who gives you a cup of water in my name because you belong to Christ will certainly not lose his reward.

Causing to Sin

⁴²"And if anyone causes one of these little ones who believe in me to sin, it would be better for him to be thrown into the sea with a large millstone tied around his neck. ⁴³If your hand causes you to sin, cut it off. It is better for you to enter life maimed than with two hands to go into hell, where the fire never goes out.⁸ ⁴⁵And if your foot causes you to sin, cut it off. It is

Questions

OPEN: 1. If you could recapture one quality you had as a child, what would it be? 2. What quality of a sibling or best friend do you wish you had?

DIG: 1. As a disciple, how would you feel when Jesus asked about the argument? What is Jesus' point in emphasizing service? In using the child as an object lesson on true greatness in the kingdom? 2. What is ironic about verses 38-41 (see 9:18)? Why are these exorcists a problem for John? 3. What does it mean to act "in Jesus' name" (see Ac 19:13-16)? 4. In verses 42-49, what four things does Jesus say are "better"? What is his point in using such hyperbole (exaggerated language)? What might be the outcome if people failed to recognize this as hyperbole? 5. How does this relate to his other teachings about discipleship in 9:33-41? In 8:34? What is critical? 6. How does the admonition to be at peace (v.50) relate to verses 42-49? 7. In 10:1-12, how were the Pharisees trying to test Jesus by their question? What was their viewpoint on divorce (see Dt 24:1-4; see also notes)? 8. Instead of answering their question, how does Jesus put them to the test by emphasizing God's intent for marriage? 9. In light of the political situation (6:17-19), what risks was Jesus taking in affirming the rights of women (vv.11-12)?

[Scripture and questions continued on page 56]

ᵍ43 Some manuscripts *out,* ⁴⁴*where /* " ' *their worm does not die, / and the fire is not quenched.'*
ʰ45 Some manuscripts *hell,* ⁴⁶*where /* " ' *their worm does not die, / and the fire is not quenched.'* ⁱ48 Isaiah 66: 24

Notes

9:33-50 In this section Jesus teaches about discipleship. Specifically, the focus of this teaching is relationships between people, i.e., how to move from argument (9:33) to peace (9:50). By comparison with where this material appears in Matthew and Luke, it would appear that once again (as he did in 4:1-34), Mark has collected into one unit teachings given by Jesus on various occasions. These sayings are linked together by various "catch words." Furthermore, the topic which began this section (the disciples arguing with each other) is resolved at the end (with the injunction in 9:50 to "be at peace with each other"). This was a common device used in the first century to aid memorization in an era when books were not widely available.

9:33-37 For the second time following the Lord's words about what will happen to him, there is an incident which demonstrates that the disciples have not grasped what he is saying (see also 8:31, followed by 8:32-33). In this case, despite Jesus' teaching about betrayal and death, the disciples continue to have visions of a literal kingdom to be established on earth with Jesus as its head. They are arguing about who will have what position in that kingdom.

9:34 *greatest*. Once again the disciples have missed the point. In the face of Jesus' teaching about suffering and death, they are concerned about their position and personal power. That such a topic should be debated was not unexpected, since concern for rank was common in those days. Rabbis disputed about who would be the greatest in the New Age. Each year the religious sect at Qumran ranked each member of the community in accord with his worthiness.

9:35 Once again (as he did in 8:35, when he spoke about losing one's life to save it), Jesus turns their understanding upside down. The real issue is not who is greatest, he says, but who serves best. Service, not power, is the prime value in his kingdom.

9:36 This is the first of several dramatized parables in Mark whereby Jesus uses an object in a symbolic way to make his point (e.g., 11:12-14, 20-21). The child is a symbol standing for Jesus' followers (in Aramaic and in Greek, the same word can be translated child or servant, thus referring back to his previous point in v.35). His point is that they must

welcome his followers. All of his followers need to be treated with respect.

9:38-41 From the issue of how to treat Jesus' disciples, Mark deals with the way to recognize these disciples. The point is that those who claim to be his followers must be accepted as such.

9:38 *John*. Following each of the three predictions of his death and resurrection, it is one of the three disciples closest to Jesus who is shown to be missing the point: Peter in 8:32, John here, and James (along with John) in 10:35-37. *a man driving out demons in your name*. Acts 19:13-16 describes the successful use by Jewish exorcists of Jesus' name to drive out demons. In exorcism, it was the power of the name that dominated (see notes on 1:24 and 5:6-9). This unnamed exorcist is an example of one of his followers who is to be welcomed (thus illustrating the point Jesus just made in v.37).

9:39-40 *Do not stop him*. The attempt by the disciples to stop this unauthorized exorcism is an abuse of their authority (demonstrating once again that this is what they are thinking about), made all the more ironic by their own failure to cast out the demon from the epileptic boy (vv.17-18).

9:41 *a cup of water*. An act of hospitality and service in a country where water was scarce and the sun burning hot.

9:42-50 Mark adds to the two previous incidents a collection of other related sayings (much as he added the sayings in 4:21-34 to the parable of the sower in 4:1-20).

9:42 *these little ones who believe in me*. The reference is to Jesus' followers (see v.37). *causes...to sin*. Lit., something which snares a person or animal; which causes them to trip up or entices them to stray. *the sea*. Jews were terrified of the sea. *a large millstone*. There are two words for millstone. One refers to a small hand mill used in a home; the other (which Jesus uses here) refers to the huge upper stone of a community mill, so big that it had to be drawn around by a donkey. Jesus uses hyperbole to make his point.

9:43 *cut it off*. Another hyperbole. That Jesus is not calling for his followers to indulge in physical

[Notes continued on page 57]   55

better for you to enter life crippled than to have two feet and be thrown into hell. *k 47*And if your eye causes you to sin, pluck it out. It is better for you to enter the kingdom of God with one eye than to have two eyes and be thrown into hell, 48where

" 'their worm does not die,
and the fire is not quenched.' *l*

49Everyone will be salted with fire.

50"Salt is good, but if it loses its saltiness, how can you make it salty again? Have salt in yourselves, and be at peace with each other."

Divorce

10 Jesus then left that place and went into the region of Judea and across the Jordan. Again crowds of people came to him, and as was his custom, he taught them.

2Some Pharisees came and tested him by asking, "Is it lawful for a man to divorce his wife?"

3"What did Moses command you?" he replied.

4They said, "Moses permitted a man to write a certificate of divorce and send her away."

5"It was because your hearts were hard that Moses wrote you this law," Jesus replied. 6"But at the beginning of creation God 'made them male and female.' *j* 7"For this reason a man will leave his father and mother and be united to his wife, *k* 8and the two will become one flesh.' *l* So they are no longer two, but one. 9Therefore what God has joined together, let man not separate."

10When they were in the house again, the disciples asked Jesus about this. 11He answered, "Anyone who divorces his wife and marries another woman commits adultery against her. 12And if she divorces her husband and marries another man, she commits adultery."

REFLECT: 1. How does success "Jesus-style" differ from the ideas of success that press on you today? What would it mean for you to reflect verses 35-37 in your family? Your work? What is the surprising incentive to do so? **2.** What Christian groups do you tend to "bad-mouth" because they are not "one of us"? Why? What is Jesus' point for you here? **3.** How can you apply the principles of marriage stressed here? **4.** Do you think Jesus would give the same response to someone in a troubled marriage who sincerely asked the question in verse 2? Why or why not?

j6 Gen. 1:27   *k7* Some early manuscripts do not have *and be united to his wife.*
l8 Gen. 2:24

Notes, continued

mutilation (which was forbidden by the OT) is demonstrated by the fact that the early Christians were not noted for being eyeless or legless. *life*. Spiritual life; life in the kingdom of God (see v.47). *hell*. Lit., Gehenna—a ravine outside Jerusalem where children were once sacrificed and where garbage was burned during the time of Jesus. Gehenna became a symbol for extreme horror, the place of punishment and spiritual death.

9:48 Gehenna is a place where horrid worms live in the refuse and where the fire smolders constantly. His point in this section is that any sacrifice is worth avoiding Gehenna.

9:49 The allusion is to the practice of sprinkling salt on the sacrifices that were to be burned on the altar (see Lev 2:13).

9:50 *salt*. Salt does not normally lose its taste, but salt from the Dead Sea was mixed with impurities and over time could acquire a stale taste. If his followers lose their salt (probably meaning their sense of servanthood—see v.35), this is not easily restored. *be at peace with each other*. However, when his followers have such a sense of service, peace is the outcome. Had the disciples grasped this concept of servanthood instead of opting for power and greatness, they would not have been arguing on the road (9:33). Thus Mark returns back to the issue which began this teaching section.

10:1-52 This chapter records the incidents en route from Capernaum to Jerusalem on Jesus' final journey, a trip that will culminate in his death.

10:1 Jesus goes south, over the hills into Samaria, following the traditional route of pilgrims on their way to Jerusalem. *that place*. He begins his journey to Jerusalem in Capernaum (see 9:33), the place where his ministry began in the Gospel of Mark (1:16-45). *Judea*. A Roman province in the south of Palestine, similar in size and location to the land of Judah in the OT. *across the Jordan*. This is a reference to a specific region called Peraea, which was a narrow corridor on the east side of the Jordan. Pious Jews would cross over the Jordan into Peraea to avoid travelling through Samaria (where they would become ritually unclean). This is the territory of Herod Antipas, the ruler who beheaded John the Baptist.

10:2 *tested him*. It is not by chance that the Pharisees question Jesus about divorce. It was this issue that led to John the Baptist's death (see 6:17-28). Perhaps they hoped that Jesus would slip up and respond in a way that would get him arrested by Herod. *divorce*. All the Jewish parties agreed (on the basis of Dt 24:1) that divorce was allowed. The issue in this debate concerned the grounds on which such divorce was permissible. The strict rabbis allowed divorce only on the basis of adultery. Liberal teachers allowed divorce for a host of reasons: e.g., if a woman spoiled her husband's dinner, or if her husband found her less attractive than someone else. In any case, it was only the husband who had the right of divorce. The most that a wife could do was to ask her husband to divorce her.

10:4 *a certificate of divorce*. This was issued to the woman as a form of protection, verifying her release from marriage and giving her the right to remarry.

10:5-9 Jesus attacks the way Deuteronomy 24:1-4 had come to be used by the religious leaders of his day. Originally its aim was to prohibit a divorced and remarried woman from remarrying her former husband. However, it came to be taken as a sanction for divorce, which in that era had become very easy for husbands to obtain. Jesus quotes from the account of creation (in Ge 1-2) to make his point that the original intention of God was an indissoluble union whereby two people become one. God joins the couple together (v.9) and they are responsible to each other for maintaining this union (vv.7-8). However, implied in Jesus' affirmation that their hearts had become hard (v.5) is the recognition that such a union can be destroyed (see Mt 5:32). In this passage, Jesus champions the rights of women in an era when they were at the mercy of their husbands. If they were divorced, they were given a single monetary settlement (unless they were guilty of adultery) which was never more than their dowry.

10:10-12 *commits adultery against her*. Once again Jesus focuses on the rights of women. Nowhere in the Jewish literature of that era can a statement like this be found. Adultery was always considered to be an offense against the man, and never against the woman.

UNIT 17 Little Children/Rich Young Man

Mark 10:13-31

The Little Children and Jesus

¹³People were bringing little children to Jesus to have him touch them, but the disciples rebuked them. ¹⁴When Jesus saw this, he was indignant. He said to them, "Let the little children come to me, and do not hinder them, for the kingdom of God belongs to such as these. ¹⁵I tell you the truth, anyone who will not receive the kingdom of God like a little child will never enter it." ¹⁶And he took the children in his arms, put his hands on them and blessed them.

The Rich Young Man

¹⁷As Jesus started on his way, a man ran up to him and fell on his knees before him. "Good teacher," he asked, "what must I do to inherit eternal life?"

¹⁸"Why do you call me good?" Jesus answered. "No one is good—except God alone. ¹⁹You know the commandments: 'Do not murder, do not commit adultery, do not steal, do not give false testimony, do not defraud, honor your father and mother.'ᵐ"

²⁰"Teacher," he declared, "all these I have kept since I was a boy."

²¹Jesus looked at him and loved him. "One thing you lack," he said. "Go, sell everything you have and give to the poor, and you will have treasure in heaven. Then come, follow me."

²²At this the man's face fell. He went away sad, because he had great wealth.

²³Jesus looked around and said to his disciples, "How hard it is for the rich to enter the kingdom of God!"

²⁴The disciples were amazed at his words. But Jesus said again, "Children, how hard it isⁿ to enter the kingdom of God! ²⁵It is easier for a camel to go through the eye of a needle than for a rich man to enter the kingdom of God."

²⁶The disciples were even more amazed, and said to each other, "Who then can be saved?"

²⁷Jesus looked at them and said, "With man this is impossible, but not with God; all things are possible with God."

²⁸Peter said to him, "We have left everything to follow you!"

²⁹"I tell you the truth," Jesus replied, "no one who has left home or brothers or sisters or mother or father or children or fields for me and the gospel ³⁰will fail to receive a hundred times as much in this present age (homes, brothers, sisters, mothers, children and fields—and with them, persecutions) and in the age to come, eternal life. ³¹But many who are first will be last, and the last first."

Questions

OPEN: 1. What really bugs you about kids? What is really great about them? **2.** When have you been given an "impossible" task? What happened?

DIG: 1. Why would the disciples want to keep the children away from Jesus? What childlike qualities was Jesus commending (vv.13-16)? How does childlikeness relate to the kingdom of God? **2.** How does the man's question (v.17) compare with what Jesus had just taught about the kingdom (v.15)? What was his assumption about how one gains the kingdom? **3.** What is Jesus trying to drive home by responding to the way the man addressed him (v.18)? **4.** Jesus quizzes the man on only a partial list of the Ten Commandments (see Ex 20). How well might the man have obeyed the ones relating directly to God? **5.** Why does Jesus command the man as he does (v.21; see also 8:34)? What does the young man's response reveal which had been hidden by his good works? **6.** Is this a general call to reduce oneself to poverty (or to simplify one's lifestyle) in order to follow Jesus? Why do you think so? **7.** What does the disciples' shock and follow-up question (v.26) reveal about them? On what basis is it possible for anyone—rich ruler or poor fisherman—to receive the kingdom? **8.** How is the promise of verses 29-30 to come true for believers? Is this a promise of worldly blessing, eternal life, or both? Why? Historically, who shall be "first" and "last" in that kingdom (v.31)?

REFLECT: 1. Are you more like the man or the children (vv.13-16) in terms of the way you approach God? Why? **2.** Supposing you could climb your way to heaven by works of the law, which rung of the ladder would you be on by now: Just starting out? Stepping on people's toes? Almost to the top? Falling off? **3.** What has helped you to see the impossibility of "earning" the kingdom? As a result, how have you experienced the gift of the kingdom as described in verses 29-30? **4.** What could Jesus point to in your life that is preventing you from receiving the kingdom? Why?

ᵐ19 Exodus 20:12-16; Deut. 5:16-20   ⁿ24 Some manuscripts *is for those who trust in riches*

Notes

10:13-16 From women and marriage, the subject moves naturally to children. Jesus affirms women and children. This was uncharacteristic of his age, in which both groups were considered to be inferior.

10:13 *little children*. Children are dependent upon others and receptive to what they are given. It is this spirit of openness and dependence that Jesus commends. **the disciples rebuked them**. The demands on Jesus were ceaseless (e.g., 6:30-31). The disciples wanted to protect him—it was understandable that they would turn away this demand.

10:14 Once again Jesus does the unexpected. He invites the weak and the helpless into his kingdom.

10:17-31 In contrast to children, Jesus next meets one who is wealthy and powerful. He turns away the rich young man with the severity of his demand.

10:17 *a man*. Luke describes him as a ruler (Lk 18:18); Matthew calls him young (Mt 19:20). **Good Teacher**. His assumption is that some people are good (and merit eternal life), while others are not. This is a distinction which Jesus does not accept. Instead, he casts the whole question into terms of dependence and openness (vv.14-15). **what must I do**. This emphasis on doing is in sharp contrast to Jesus' teaching about receiving the kingdom as a gift that is grasped by faith (see 10:15). **inherit**. Gain entrance to; possess. **eternal life**. What he is asking for is entrance to the kingdom of God (see vv.23,25).

10:18 In the OT only God is called "good" (see v. 17). Does this young man really grasp what is implied in this title that he so easily gives to Jesus?

10:19 *the commandments*. Those which Jesus lists all come from the Ten Commandments, with the exception of "do not defraud."

10:20 He kept the commandments, yet he is unsure whether he has gained eternal life. This was the insecurity of a system based on works-righteousness. **since I was a boy**. A Jewish boy was responsible from age 13 onward to keep the commandments.

10:21 *loved him*. Mark is the only Gospel to note Jesus' affection for this earnest and sincere young man. **Go, sell everything**. It was felt in the OT that riches by themselves were no hindrance to spiritual pursuit. But Jesus points out that accumulation of wealth can hinder participation in God's kingdom. This is not a general call to poverty in order to follow Jesus, as is evident from his other teachings. By telling the young man to sell all his goods, it became evident to the youth that his faith was in his possessions, not Jesus. Since he will not change his mind (repent), he walks away. **follow me**. The emphasis is not on the selling all, but on the following of Jesus.

10:24 *amazed*. The disciples are astonished because traditional Jewish wisdom saw wealth as a sign of God's favor (e.g., Job 1:10, 42:10; Ps 128:1-2). **how hard it is**. Jesus repeats his statement, but now drops the reference to the rich.

10:25 Once again Jesus makes his point by using humorous hyperbole. The camel was the largest animal in Palestine, and certainly couldn't get through the smallest opening known to most people ("the eye of a needle"). Contrary to popular belief, there was no gate into Jerusalem called "The Needle's Eye."

10:26 *even more amazed*. The disciples are even more bewildered than before. What Jesus says directly confronts their assumptions about salvation. **Who then can be saved?** They realize the radical nature of Jesus' statement and wonder about their own fate. If it is difficult for anyone to enter the kingdom, then what chance have they got?

10:27 This is Jesus' point. It is, indeed, impossible for a man to make his own way into the kingdom. It is God who grants this gift.

10:29 *for me and the gospel*. That for which the sacrifice of leaving home and family is made is Jesus and the work of his kingdom.

10:30 There is a certain irony in Jesus' words. Those who leave a settled life to follow Jesus will be given a new place, a new family, and the support from new fields. That this is not to be taken as a promise of worldly blessing is made clear by Mark's addition of "persecutions" as part of what they will gain.

10:31 Once again Jesus reverses expectations. Many (but not all) of those who think they are worthy of God's favor will find that they do not have it; while many of those who are at the bottom (e.g., tax collectors, sinners) will gain that favor. This pithy statement by Jesus is used here as a summary of his teaching on discipleship in this section (9:33-10:31).

UNIT 18   Jesus Predicts His Death Again/Request of James and John/Blind Bartimaeus

Mark 10:32-52

Jesus Again Predicts His Death

³²They were on their way up to Jerusalem, with Jesus leading the way, and the disciples were astonished, while those who followed were afraid. Again he took the Twelve aside and told them what was going to happen to him. ³³"We are going up to Jerusalem," he said, "and the Son of Man will be betrayed to the chief priests and teachers of the law. They will condemn him to death and will hand him over to the Gentiles, ³⁴who will mock him and spit on him, flog him and kill him. Three days later he will rise."

The Request of James and John

³⁵Then James and John, the sons of Zebedee, came to him. "Teacher," they said, "we want you to do for us whatever we ask."

³⁶"What do you want me to do for you?" he asked.

³⁷They replied, "Let one of us sit at your right and the other at your left in your glory."

³⁸"You don't know what you are asking," Jesus said. "Can you drink the cup I drink or be baptized with the baptism I am baptized with?"

³⁹"We can," they answered.

Jesus said to them, "You will drink the cup I drink and be baptized with the baptism I am baptized with, ⁴⁰but to sit at my right or left is not for me to grant. These places belong to those for whom they have been prepared."

⁴¹When the ten heard about this, they became indignant with James and John. ⁴²Jesus called them together and said, "You know that those who are regarded as rulers of the Gentiles lord it over them, and their high officials exercise authority over them. ⁴³Not so with you. Instead, whoever wants to become great among you must be your servant, ⁴⁴and whoever wants to be first must be slave of all. ⁴⁵For even the Son of Man did not come to be served, but to serve, and to give his life as a ransom for many."

Questions

OPEN: 1. What is the scariest journey that you remember? **2.** What famous person would you like to be the "right-hand man" (or woman) for?

DIG: 1. Why would going to Jerusalem cause the disciples to be astonished and afraid? **2.** What impresses you about Jesus' resolve with the Twelve and with James and John? **3.** What view of the kingdom are James and John still clinging to? How could they respond like this in light of verses 33-34? **4.** What is "the cup" and "the baptism" and the "glory" as each applies to Jesus? To the disciples? **5.** What made the other disciples indignant? **6.** How does Jesus use this uproar to convey new insights about what greatness is all about? **7.** How does Jesus practice what he preached? In this context, what is a "ransom for many"? How is the death of Christ the ultimate service to all? **8.** How does 10:45 answer the question in 8:37? **9.** In verses 46-52, what is significant about the title Bartimaeus uses for Jesus as he prepares to enter Jerusalem? **10.** How does Bartimaeus demonstrate faith which the crowd lacked? **11.** How is Bartimaeus different from the young man in 10:17-22? **12.** Why is there no "order of silence," as in 7:36? **13.** What is the significance of this healing for the Twelve (see notes)?

[Scripture and questions continued on page 62]

Notes

10:32-34 For the the third and final time, Jesus predicts his death and resurrection. This is the fullest of his three predictions. In addition to what he has already said, he points out *where* these events will take place (Jerusalem) and what the *role of the Gentiles* will be (they will torment him and then do the actual killing). The progression from condemnation to mocking, being spit on, flogging, and finally death makes clear that the focus of coming events is his death.

10:32 Jerusalem. Jesus' destination is now revealed as is the site of his betrayal, death, and resurrection (see v.33).

10:35-45 The three predictions of his passion (8:31; 9:31; 10:33-34) are followed by three failures of the disciples to understand what he is saying (8:32-33; 9:32-34; 10:35-40), followed in turn by three teaching sessions in which Jesus explains what discipleship means (8:34-38; 9:35-37; 10:42-45).

10:35 James and John. Perhaps it is because they are closest to Jesus that they presume to make such a request.

10:37 They expect that Jesus will come into a position of authority as the new king of Israel. (This was the general assumption in those days about the Messiah.) Those who sit on his right and his left will be his chief lieutenants.

10:38 drink this cup. This is a phrase which means "share the same fate." In the OT, the cup is a metaphor for wrath (e.g., Ps 75:8 and Isa 51:17-22). **baptism**. In the OT, the image of a deluge or flood overwhelming one is used as a metaphor for disaster (e.g., Ps 42:7 and Isa 43:2). Both the cup and the baptism refer to Jesus' coming suffering and death for the sins of the world. Both would remind Mark's readers of the sacraments of communion and baptism and help them understand that to participate in these is to open themselves up to suffering and death—an apt word for those facing death in the coliseum.

10:39-40 Their leadership will not be expressed through positions of authority, but through suffering and death. **We can**. The disciples answer too readily Jesus' question as to whether they can share his cup and his baptism. They do not grasp what he means by this question, thinking perhaps that it is referring to being in fellowship with him.

10:41 they became indignant. As self-serving as the request of James and John had been, the response of the ten is not much better. They get angry when they hear what happened. James and John want to have positions ahead of them! All twelve share the same view of the kingdom, it seems, namely that it will be earthly and political, with Jesus as the reigning king and them as his chief lieutenants (as is seen in what Jesus has to say to them in 10:42-45).

10:42-45 With this final statement, Mark ends this long section (which began in 8:31) in which Jesus is shown primarily in his role as teacher. Jesus' teaching has been structured around three attempts to get the disciples to understand what kind of Messiah he is. In the course of doing this, he teaches them what it means to be his disciple. His words here sum up what he has said: in the same way that the Messiah came to serve, so too must his disciples. They are not to seek power and authority over others, but rather they are to serve them.

10:43 servant. Rather than become masters (and exercise authority), they are to become servants (and meet the needs of others). The Greek word for servant (*diakonos*, from which the English word "deacon" is derived) became the most common description of church leaders in the early church.

10:45 Jesus now reveals why he must suffer and die. It is in order to redeem the many. This statement of Jesus also defines the theme of the final section of his Gospel (which begins in a few verses): the suffering and death of Jesus on behalf of humanity. **ransom**. In the first century, a slave or a prisoner could gain freedom if a purchase price (ransom) was paid. Jesus would pay the ransom price "for many" by his death (see Tit 2:14; 1Pe 1:18-19).

10:46-52 There is one final event that must take place before the start of holy week (the last week of Jesus' life). The disciples need a second touch so that they can see clearly the meaning of the coming events. They are like the man healed at Bethsaida (8:22-26): they have begun to see

[Notes continued on page 63]

Mark 10:32-52, continued

Questions

Blind Bartimaeus Receives His Sight

[46]Then they came to Jericho. As Jesus and his disciples, together with a large crowd, were leaving the city, a blind man, Bartimaeus (that is, the Son of Timaeus), was sitting by the roadside begging. [47]When he heard that it was Jesus of Nazareth, he began to shout, "Jesus, Son of David, have mercy on me!"

[48]Many rebuked him and told him to be quiet, but he shouted all the more, "Son of David, have mercy on me!"

[49]Jesus stopped and said, "Call him."

So they called to the blind man, "Cheer up! On your feet! He's calling you." [50]Throwing his cloak aside, he jumped to his feet and came to Jesus.

[51]"What do you want me to do for you?" Jesus asked him.

The blind man said, "Rabbi, I want to see."

[52]"Go," said Jesus, "your faith has healed you." Immediately he received his sight and followed Jesus along the road.

REFLECT: 1. How and why do you find yourself desiring the first chair in God's orchestra? **2.** How does Jesus' life as a servant influence your view of spiritual power? Your relationships? Your use of your gifts? **3.** What one way could you serve this week? **4.** If Jesus asked you, "What do you want me to do for you?", what would you say? What would be your part and God's part in fulfilling your desire?

Notes, continued

again but their vision is fuzzy. They see that Jesus is the Messiah, but they do not see what kind of Messiah he is (as Mark has just shown). So here, once again, Mark uses a healing in a symbolic way. The healing of blind Bartimaeus signals the second touch of healing that will cure the blindness of the Twelve.

10:46 *Jericho*. They have almost completed their journey from Galilee (see 9:33; 10:1). Jericho is a city some 18 miles east of Jerusalem and the place where travellers recrossed the Jordan back into Israel. ***a large crowd***. These were pilgrims on their way to Jerusalem for the Passover Feast. Every male over 12 years of age living within a 15-mile radius of Jerusalem was expected to attend.

10:47 *Jesus, Son of David*. A debate was going on as to who the Messiah would be. Would he come from the tribe of Levi, or was he a king in the line of David? Clearly this is a Messianic title by which Bartimaeus hails Jesus. Interestingly, Jesus does not silence him as he has done so often in the past when his identity is revealed. The time for secrecy is past. He accepts the title. This is the only use in Mark of this particular title: on the eve of Jesus' entry into Jerusalem as messianic king.

10:52 *your faith has healed you*. Bartimaeus demonstrated his faith in several ways: by his title for Jesus (showing that he grasped who Jesus was), by his persistence (he will not let this opportunity go by), and by his request for healing (showing that he believed Jesus could do so).

UNIT 19 Triumphal Entry/Jesus Clears the Temple/ Withered Fig Tree

Mark 11:1-25

The Triumphal Entry

11 As they approached Jerusalem and came to Bethphage and Bethany at the Mount of Olives, Jesus sent two of his disciples, ²saying to them, "Go to the village ahead of you, and just as you enter it, you will find a colt tied there, which no one has ever ridden. Untie it and bring it here. ³If anyone asks you, 'Why are you doing this?' tell him, 'The Lord needs it and will send it back here shortly.' "

⁴They went and found a colt outside in the street, tied at a doorway. As they untied it, ⁵some people standing there asked, "What are you doing, untying that colt?" ⁶They answered as Jesus had told them to, and the people let them go. ⁷When they brought the colt to Jesus and threw their cloaks over it, he sat on it. ⁸Many people spread their cloaks on the road, while others spread branches they had cut in the fields. ⁹Those who went ahead and those who followed shouted,

"Hosanna!ᵒ"

"Blessed is he who comes in the name of the Lord!"ᵖ

¹⁰"Blessed is the coming kingdom of our father David!"

"Hosanna in the highest!"

¹¹Jesus entered Jerusalem and went to the temple. He looked around at everything, but since it was already late, he went out to Bethany with the Twelve.

Questions

OPEN: If you were the advance man for the Messiah, what kind of entry would you have planned?

DIG: 1. How did the manner in which Jesus entered Jerusalem confirm his character (see Zec 9:9; 14:4-5)? Why a colt and not a war horse? What tells you that Jesus is choreographing this event from start to finish? **2.** In light of the response he received, what were the expectations of the crowd? Of the disciples (see 10:37)? Of Jesus? **3.** What do you find most significant about the triumphal entry into Jerusalem? **4.** How does the story of the fig tree relate to the clearing of the temple (vv.13-14,20-21)? In what ways did the Pharisees cover their fruitlessness with flashy foliage? **5.** This profiteering on the sale of sacrificial animals took place in the only area where Gentiles could worship. Why would that especially anger Jesus (see Isa 56:6-8)? What was Jesus threatening when he called the temple a "den of robbers" (see Jer 7:9-15)? What does this event show you about Jesus? **6.** Why did the priests and teachers have to be so crafty in their plot? **7.** From verses 20-21, why was Peter surprised? What conditions for effective prayer are listed here (vv.22-25)?

[Scripture and questions continued on page 66]

ᵒ9 A Hebrew expression meaning "Save!" which became an exclamation of praise; also in verse 10   ᵖ9 Psalm 118:25,26

Notes

11:1-16:8 All of the remaining events in the Gospel of Mark occur in and around Jerusalem (much of it in the Temple area) during the last week of Jesus' life.

11:1-11 As the final chapter opens in Mark's account of Jesus, a new note is sounded: openness. Jesus so arranges his entry into Jerusalem (and it is clear that it is Jesus who is choreographing this event) that he arrives, openly, as the Messiah. The time for secrecy is past. His whole arrival rings of the Messiah from fulfilled prophecy (Zec 9:9 and esp. 14:4) and royal greetings (e.g., 2Ki 9:13) to cries to God to "Save now."

11:1 *Jerusalem*. This was the central city in Palestine and spiritual heart of Israel. ***Bethany***. A small village some two miles east of Jerusalem, site of the eastern slope of the Mount of Olives. This is where Jesus and his disciples were lodged during the Passover. ***Mount of Olives***. This place was associated in popular understanding with the coming of the Messiah. According to Zechariah 14:4-5, this is the place where God will commence the final judgment of Israel's enemies. It is not by accident that Jesus chose this place to prepare his entry into Jerusalem. ***Jesus sent***. Having come to the right spot, his next step is to send two disciples to secure the colt on which he will ride into Jerusalem. Clearly Jesus is consciously preparing his entry. His arrival will reveal who he is.

11:2 *a colt*. According to Zechariah 9:9, the King would come riding on a colt. Jesus will not simply enter Jerusalem. He will come as the Messianic King. However, he will not come as a Warrior-King (as the people expected) riding a war horse. ***tied there***. Genesis 49:8-12 speaks of a tethered colt, and this was understood by many to be a prophecy of the Messiah. ***which no one has ridden***. This colt had never been put to ordinary use and so was ideal for this very special purpose (see Nu 19:2; 1Sa 6:7-8).

11:8 *spread their cloaks*. This was a gesture of respect, given to kings (see 2Ki 9:12-13). Blind Bartimaeus has declared him the Son of David, and now the people treat him as such.

11:9-10 The shouts of joy were typical of pilgrims en route to Jerusalem for a feast. Here it adds to the prophetic sense of what was taking place. This time the real King is, indeed, arriving in the Holy City. How many recognized this fact is difficult to assess. Still, by enacting this ancient ritual, they were (unknowingly for many) welcoming the true King. ***Hosanna!*** Lit., "Save now." The Psalm from which this cry is taken (Ps 118:25-26) was understood by the rabbis to be a Messianic psalm, referring to King David and the final redemption.

11:11 *temple*. This was the third temple to be built on Mount Zion. It was built by Herod the Great in 20 B.C. and was a magnificent structure covering some 30 acres. The temple consisted of four concentric courts ringed by enormous walls.

11:12-21 Once again Mark sandwiches together two stories: the cursing of the fig tree and the cleansing of the temple. Each story helps interpret the other. Both illustrate the judgment that is coming on Jerusalem.

11:13 *fig tree*. On the Mount of Olives, fig trees are in leaf by early April, but they would not have ripe fruit until June, long after the Passover. Fig trees were a common prophetic symbol. They were associated with Israel and with judgment (e.g., Hos 9:10-11; Jer 8:13; Mic 7:1).

11:14 *his disciples heard him say it*. Jesus has done something so seemingly out of character (cursing a fig tree for not doing what it could not do) that the disciples cannot help but notice. Since there is no obvious reason for his action (Mark has taken care to point out that "it was not the season for figs"), they are forced to ponder why he did this. In the same way that he often used extravagant language to make his point (e.g., 9:42-43), here Jesus uses extravagant actions to get across this crucial point. Such acted-out parables were very much a part of how the OT prophets communicated (see, for example, Isa 20 and Eze 4-5).

11:15-19 Jesus' first act following his triumphal entry is to go into the temple and (by his actions) call to account the religious leadership of Israel. It is significant that he challenges these leaders in the temple, the very center of their power. Once again Jesus conveys his message by means of dramatic action.

[Notes continued on page 67]

Mark 11:1-25, continued

Questions

Jesus Clears the Temple

[12]The next day as they were leaving Bethany, Jesus was hungry. [13]Seeing in the distance a fig tree in leaf, he went to find out if it had any fruit. When he reached it, he found nothing but leaves, because it was not the season for figs. [14]Then he said to the tree, "May no one ever eat fruit from you again." And his disciples heard him say it.

[15]On reaching Jerusalem, Jesus entered the temple area and began driving out those who were buying and selling there. He overturned the tables of the money changers and the benches of those selling doves, [16]and would not allow anyone to carry merchandise through the temple courts. [17]And as he taught them, he said, "Is it not written:

" 'My house will be called
a house of prayer for all nations'[q]?

But you have made it 'a den of robbers.'[r]'"

[18]The chief priests and the teachers of the law heard this and began looking for a way to kill him, for they feared him, because the whole crowd was amazed at his teaching.

[19]When evening came, they[s] went out of the city.

The Withered Fig Tree

[20]In the morning, as they went along, they saw the fig tree withered from the roots. [21]Peter remembered and said to Jesus, "Rabbi, look! The fig tree you cursed has withered!"

[22]"Have[t] faith in God," Jesus answered. [23]"I tell you the truth, if anyone says to this mountain, 'Go, throw yourself into the sea,' and does not doubt in his heart but believes that what he says will happen, it will be done for him. [24]Therefore I tell you, whatever you ask for in prayer, believe that you have received it, and it will be yours. [25]And when you stand praying, if you hold anything against anyone, forgive him, so that your Father in heaven may forgive you your sins.[u]"

REFLECT: 1. How did Jesus ride into your life: As a conquering hero forcing you into submission? As a gentle king bearing peace? As a white knight rescuing you? How about now? **2.** Have you ever misunderstood Jesus' purposes, praising him one day and despairing the next? What was the basis for your misunderstanding? **3.** Where is your "Jerusalem"—the destiny or fulfillment of your life? Where along that road to your Jerusalem are you now? **4.** If you were a tree, what would help you produce more fruit: Pruning? Watering? Staking? Transplanting? Fertilizing? Why? **5.** What does this story and 9:42 show you about what angers Jesus most? How could this relate to your religious practices?

[q]17 Isaiah 56:7   [r]17 Jer. 7:11   [s]19 Some early manuscripts he   [t]22 Some early manuscripts If you have   [u]25 Some manuscripts sins. [26]But if you do not forgive, neither will your Father who is in heaven forgive your sins.

Notes, continued

11:15 *buying and selling*. Worship in the temple centered on sacrifice. Those wishing to participate were required to offer an unblemished animal, and apparently temple inspectors approved only those animals bought from certified vendors (who sold animals at a huge markup). During this era, these merchants worked for members of the High Priest's family. There was profiteering on the part of priests and others, who were taking advantage of the religious obligations of the people. ***money changers***. At Passover, each Jew was required to pay a temple tax of one-half shekel (nearly two days' wages). No other currency was acceptable. Those who changed the various Roman coins into shekels charged exorbitant amounts for this simple act: up to one-half day's wage. ***those selling doves***. A dove was the sacrifice offered by the poorest of people. Yet they had to pay the temple vendors some twenty times what a dove cost elsewhere.

11:16 Jesus was simply enforcing a recognized rule from the Mishnah: "A man may not enter into the temple mount with his staff or his sandal or his wallet, or with the dust upon his feet, nor may he make of it a short by-path."

11:17 *a house of prayer for all nations*. The outermost area of the temple where all these activities were taking place was called the Court of the Gentiles. It was intended to be a place where pious Gentiles could pray. Instead it had been turned into a raucous oriental bazaar, making prayer impossible and thus doing away with the only place in the temple where non-Jews could come before the true God.

11:20 *the fig tree withered from the roots*. In light of the cleansing of the temple, the meaning of the withered fig tree becomes clear. This is what will happen to Israel. Judgment is coming on Jerusalem and on the temple in particular. "Just as the leaves of the tree concealed the fact that there was no fruit to enjoy, so too the magnificence of the Temple and its ceremony conceals the fact that Israel has not brought forth the fruit of righteousness demanded by God" (Lane). (See also Mk 7:6.) The fig tree's fate will be the temple's fate. (The temple was, in fact, destroyed in A.D. 70.)

11:22-26 As he has done in the past (see 4:21-34; 9:42-50), Mark adds to the main story a group of similar sayings (this time on the subject of faith and prayer).

11:23-24 Jesus continues his use of extravagant language. He cannot literally and mechanically mean that whatever is asked will happen. This would turn prayer into magic and God into a cosmic bellhop, attending to the whim of even evil and selfish people. Still, the point is not to be missed: believing prayer is answered.

UNIT 20 Authority of Jesus Questioned/ Parable of the Tenants

Mark 11:27-12:12

The Authority of Jesus Questioned

27They arrived again in Jerusalem, and while Jesus was walking in the temple courts, the chief priests, the teachers of the law and the elders came to him. 28"By what authority are you doing these things?" they asked. "And who gave you authority to do this?"

29Jesus replied, "I will ask you one question. Answer me, and I will tell you by what authority I am doing these things. 30John's baptism—was it from heaven, or from men? Tell me!"

31They discussed it among themselves and said, "If we say, 'From heaven,' he will ask, 'Then why didn't you believe him?' 32But if we say, 'From men'. . . ." (They feared the people, for everyone held that John really was a prophet.)

33So they answered Jesus, "We don't know."

Jesus said, "Neither will I tell you by what authority I am doing these things."

The Parable of the Tenants

12 He then began to speak to them in parables: "A man planted a vineyard. He put a wall around it, dug a pit for the winepress and built a watchtower. Then he rented the vineyard to some farmers and went away on a journey. 2At harvest time he sent a servant to the tenants to collect from them some of the fruit of the vineyard. 3But they seized him, beat him and sent him away empty-handed. 4Then he sent another servant to them; they struck this man on the head and treated him shamefully. 5He sent still another, and that one they killed. He sent many others; some of them they beat, others they killed.

6"He had one left to send, a son, whom he loved. He sent him last of all, saying, 'They will respect my son.'

7"But the tenants said to one another, 'This is the heir. Come, let's kill him, and the inheritance will be ours.' 8So they took him and killed him, and threw him out of the vineyard.

9"What then will the owner of the vineyard do? He will come and kill those tenants and give the vineyard to others. 10Haven't you read this scripture:

" 'The stone the builders rejected
   has become the capstone*v*;
11the Lord has done this,
   and it is marvelous in our eyes'*w*?"

12Then they looked for a way to arrest him because they knew he had spoken the parable against them. But they were afraid of the crowd; so they left him and went away.

Questions

OPEN: 1. Do you always believe what your doctor tells you? Why or why not? **2.** How do you react to authority when you get a traffic ticket?

DIG: 1. Why were the leaders concerned about authority? In their eyes, who had legitimate authority? **2.** What dilemma does this question pose for Jesus? Why doesn't he answer them directly? **3.** Why were the leaders reluctant to say that John's authority came from man? Why don't they admit that it was from God? **4.** How does Jesus cause the leaders' trickery to backfire on them? **5.** In the Parable of the tenants, what does the vineyard represent (compare the vineyard in Isa 5:1-7)? Who is the owner? The son? Who are the tenants? The servants? What was Jesus prophesying by telling this story? **6.** How does the Scripture Jesus quotes relate to the parable (see notes)? Who were the builders? Who is the capstone? **7.** What impact did this parable have on its hearers? How did it answer the question about Jesus' authority (11:28)?

REFLECT: 1. In what way does the honor of God compete with "the praise of men" in your life? **2.** Is there a time in your life when you can identify with Jesus' sense of rejection? How so? **3.** How do you make Jesus feel welcome in your life each day? What actions might make him feel unwelcome? **4.** Does Jesus seem more like a *millstone* (weight) or a *capstone* (one who holds everything together) in your life? Why?

---

*v*10 Or *cornerstone*   *w*11 Psalm 118:22,23

68

Notes

11:27-12:40 Mark begins a second cycle of stories in which the various of religious leaders confront Jesus one by one. Each of the major groups oppose him—the Sanhedrin, which included the chief priests (11:27-33) and the teachers of the law (12:28-40); the Pharisees (12:13-17); the Herodians (12:13-17); and the Sadducees (12:18-27). These encounters parallel the first set of conflict stories found in 2:1-3:6.

11:27 *the chief priests, the teachers of the law and the elders*. The chief priests were the key officers of the temple, just below the High Priest in rank. The elders were powerful and (reputedly) wise leaders of Israel. They were generally not priests. The teachers of the law were religious lawyers (see note on 2:6). Taken together, these three groups were the Sanhedrin—the ruling Jewish council—who opposed him as Jesus prophesied they would (see 8:31).

11:28 They ask the key question: what right does Jesus have to do what he did in the temple? While not a subtle question, it was still a trap. If Jesus said he acted on his own authority, they could detain him as a hopeless megalomaniac. If he said that his authority comes from God, then they could accuse him of blasphemy, for which the penalty was death.

11:29-30 *I will ask you one question*. Answering a question with a question was common in rabbinic debate. Jesus' question puts them in the same no-win situation they try to put him in (see vv.31-32). However, this was a real question. Their view of John will determine how they feel about Jesus, since John clearly pointed to him as the Coming One.

11:31-32 They know that no matter how they answer, Jesus' point will be made, not their own. To accept that John's authority comes from God is to admit that John was a true prophet. If this were so, then they would also have had to accept that Jesus comes from God, as John said. On the other hand, to say that John just pretended to be a prophet was to court disfavor with the crowds in this public debate.

11:33 Rather than commit themselves, they profess ignorance. Thus Jesus does not have to answer their question, which was not a sincere question anyway.

12:1-12 Rather than withdrawing from the conflict, Jesus keeps up the pressure. The point of this parable is that the leaders of Israel have rejected God's messengers and so can expect judgment.

12:1 The parable of the tenants is the closest Jesus comes in his teaching to an allegory. ***vineyard***. Grapes were one of the major crops in Israel. They were eaten fresh, made into raisins, boiled into a syrup, or made into wine. Isaiah used the symbol of the vineyard in one of his prophecies. He describes Israel as a vineyard that produced only bad fruit (Isa 5:1-7). The difference between Isaiah's prophecy and Jesus' parable is that Isaiah spoke of an unresponsive vineyard (the nation of Israel), whereas Jesus identified the problem as evil tenants (the leaders of the nation). ***went away***. Absentee landlords were common in Galilee. Such a landlord would get tenant-farmers to work his large estate, requiring part of their harvest in payment for using the land. The tenant-farmers often resented the landlord.

12:2 *servant*. In this parable, the servants represent the OT prophets. In the OT, prophets were often referred to in this way (see Jer 7:25-26; Zec 1:6).

12:6 *a son whom he loved*. The crowd didn't know the identity of the son, yet Mark's readers know that it is Jesus. A central theme in Mark 11-16 is the discovery that Jesus is the Son of God. Here is the first hint (though God has declared him to be such, using the very phrase found here—see 1:11 and 9:7).

12:7 *inheritance*. The arrival of the son signaled to the tenants that the owner had died. By law, a piece of ownerless property (which it would be if they killed the son) could be kept by those who first seized it.

12:9 The appearance of the owner would shatter the illusion that the tenants now owned the land. The owner could enlist the aid of the government to force the evil tenants off his land.

12:10 *capstone*. The reference is to a stone that was rejected in the building of Solomon's temple, which was later found to be the keystone to the porch (a keystone held an arch in place). Rabbis had interpreted the stone in Psalm 118:22-23 (which Jesus quotes) to refer to Abraham, David, or the Messiah. Here the stone is Jesus (the Messiah) whom the builders (the leaders) fail to recognize.

12:12 The leaders knew exactly what part they played in Jesus' parable. They were the evil tenants who killed the servants and the heir. From their point of view, such teaching had to be stopped; yet again because of the crowds, they could do nothing.

UNIT 21 Paying Taxes/Marriage at the Resurrection/Greatest Commandment/ Who's Son is Christ/Widow's Offering

Mark 12:13-44

Questions

Paying Taxes to Caesar

¹³Later they sent some of the Pharisees and Herodians to Jesus to catch him in his words. ¹⁴They came to him and said, "Teacher, we know you are a man of integrity. You aren't swayed by men, because you pay no attention to who they are; but you teach the way of God in accordance with the truth. Is it right to pay taxes to Caesar or not? ¹⁵Should we pay or shouldn't we?"

But Jesus knew their hypocrisy. "Why are you trying to trap me?" he asked. "Bring me a denarius and let me look at it." ¹⁶They brought the coin, and he asked them, "Whose portrait is this? And whose inscription?"

"Caesar's," they replied.

¹⁷Then Jesus said to them, "Give to Caesar what is Caesar's and to God what is God's."

And they were amazed at him.

Marriage at the Resurrection

¹⁸Then the Sadducees, who say there is no resurrection, came to him with a question. ¹⁹"Teacher," they said, "Moses wrote for us that if a man's brother dies and leaves a wife but no children, the man must marry the widow and have children for his brother. ²⁰Now there were seven brothers. The first one married and died without leaving any children. ²¹The second one married the widow, but he also died, leaving no child. It was the same with the third. ²²In fact, none of the seven left any children. Last of all, the woman died too. ²³At the resurrection ˣ whose wife will she be, since the seven were married to her?"

²⁴Jesus replied, "Are you not in error because you do not know the Scriptures or the power of God? ²⁵When the dead rise, they will neither marry nor be given in marriage; they will be like the angels in heaven. ²⁶Now about the dead rising—have you not read in the book of Moses, in the account of the bush, how God said to him, 'I am the God of Abraham, the God of Isaac, and the God of Jacob'ʸ? ²⁷He is not the God of the dead, but of the living. You are badly mistaken!"

OPEN: When do you feel right about paying taxes? For what?

DIG: 1. What was dangerous about this trap? Why do the liberal Herodians (allied to Rome) and the conservative Pharisees make strange partners? How was Jesus a threat to each? **2.** What if Jesus had simply said yes? If he had said no? What did Jesus' answer probably do to their partnership? **3.** In verses 18-27, why was the Sadducees' question an odd one? Why did they ask it? **4.** What did Jesus say is the source of the Sadducees' erroneous assumption? **5.** What characterizes "resurrection life"? How does Exodus 3:6 (quoted in v.26) demonstrate the fact of the resurrection? **6.** In verses 28-34, why are these two commandments the greatest? How do the Ten Commandments relate to these two? **7.** How was this teacher unlike many others who questioned Jesus (11:28; 12:13-14, 18-19)? What does Jesus' response teach you about love (see notes)? About the kingdom? **8.** Why do you think Jesus' answer silenced his enemies? What were they thinking? **9.** In verses 35-37, what issue lies behind Jesus' question? How will the answer to this question answer all the others directed at Jesus in 11:27–12:34? What new insight does this give? **10.** How would you recognize the "strut" of these teachers of the law (vv.38-40)? By contrast, what does the "strut" of a Christian look like (see 10:42-45)? **11.** What "delights" you about this Jesus? **12.** In verses 41-44, what is Jesus' point? When is "more" actually "less"? When is a "little" a "lot"?

[Scripture and questions continued on page 72]

ˣ23 Some manuscripts *resurrection, when men rise from the dead,*   ʸ26 Exodus 3:6

Notes

12:13-17 Beaten badly in their first two confrontations with Jesus, the leaders regroup and consider their strategy. They decide to send representatives from two groups with a trick question they hope will trap Jesus. The question deals with the explosive issue of taxes. If Jesus says that the people should *not* pay taxes to Caesar, then the Roman guard will arrest him for sedition. On the other hand, if Jesus says they *should* pay, then he will lose his popular support. Without the crowd's protection, the leaders would have a better chance of dealing with him.

12:13 *Pharisees and Herodians*. See notes on 2:18 and 3:6. The origin of this unusual alliance is described in Mk 3:1-6.

12:14 *you are a man of integrity*. By these and other flattering words they hope to catch Jesus off guard. ***taxes***. A poll tax had to be paid to the Romans each year by all adult Jews. This tax was deeply resented. At least one anti-tax rebellion had already been crushed. Many Jews felt that since God was the only rightful ruler of Israel, paying taxes would acknowledge the legitimacy of Caesar's rule.

12:15 *hypocrisy*. Jesus knew they were not sincere. This is the essence of hypocrisy: saying one thing while believing another (see note on 7:6). ***Bring me a denarius***. The stricter Jews would not even handle these coins. By asking for a coin, Jesus shows that he didn't carry it. A denarius was a small, silver coin (worth about 25 cents today) bearing the picture of Tiberius Caesar and a description of him as "Son of the Divine Augustine"—a man touched with divinity. (This description made the coins doubly offensive to the monotheistic Jews.) The denarius was the only coin that could be used to pay the poll tax.

12:17 Jesus' answer is profound. He grants the legitimacy of governments to collect taxes while at the same time limiting the power of governments. One's final loyalty must be to God and not to the state.

12:18-27 A third group (the Sadducees) attempts to discredit Jesus with another trick question. This time the strategy is one of ridicule.

12:18 *Sadducees*. There is little information available about this group. It seems that they were a small but highly influential party of wealthy, aristocratic priests. The High Priest was often a Sadducee. The Sadducees accepted relatively few theological doctrines. For example, they accepted only the first five books of the OT as authoritative. They also rejected the oral tradition (which put them at odds with the Pharisees). This is their first appearance in Mark's narrative, because up to this point, Jesus has been no threat to the Sadducees. However, when he cleared the temple, he invaded their sphere of influence and so became their enemy. ***resurrection***. The belief that at the end of the age God would bring the dead back to life.

12:19-23 The question they pose has to do with so-called "levirate marriage" (see Dt 25:5-10), which was designed to ensure the continuation of the family name, as well as to keep property within a family.

12:24-27 Jesus takes their question seriously (although it is not a sincere question, since they did not believe in the resurrection) and answers them directly. In so doing, he affirms belief in the resurrection. His own resurrection will take place within a week.

12:25 Jesus indicates that resurrection life will be radically different—more like the experience of angels than the social and physical laws at work now.

12:26 Jesus affirms the fact of the resurrection in a manner which, though strange to modern ears, was convincing to a first-century rabbi. His argument is that if God is still the God of the patriarchs (God says "I *am* the God of Abraham," using the present tense), then the patriarchs must be alive. The implication is that there will be a resurrection. Jesus draws his proof from Exodus 3:6, a portion of the OT which was accepted as authoritative by the Sadducees.

12:28 *teachers of the law*. Jesus has answered successfully the Herodians, the Pharisees, and the Sadducees. It is now a Scribe's turn to ask a question. (See notes on 2:6 and 11:27 for this group.) His attitude toward Jesus is different from the others. He asks a genuine question. ***noticing that Jesus had given a good answer***. This teacher of the law is apparently very impressed with the way Jesus answered the questions, so he asks an important question for him personally. ***which is the most important***. This phrase is, lit., "which is the chief (or first) commandment"; i.e., what commandment summarizes all the commandments. Such a question was typical of one of the two tendencies in that day when it came to the law. The majority group (represented by the Pharisees) sought to expand the law

[Notes continued on page 73]   71

Mark 12:13-44, continued

Questions

The Greatest Commandment

[28]One of the teachers of the law came and heard them debating. Noticing that Jesus had given them a good answer, he asked him, "Of all the commandments, which is the most important?" [29]"The most important one," answered Jesus, "is this: 'Hear, O Israel, the Lord our God, the Lord is one.[z] [30]Love the Lord your God with all your heart and with all your soul and with all your mind and with all your strength.'[a] [31]The second is this: 'Love your neighbor as yourself.'[b] There is no commandment greater than these."

[32]"Well said, teacher," the man replied. "You are right in saying that God is one and there is no other but him. [33]To love him with all your heart, with all your understanding and with all your strength, and to love your neighbor as yourself is more important than all burnt offerings and sacrifices."

[34]When Jesus saw that he had answered wisely, he said to him, "You are not far from the kingdom of God." And from then on no one dared ask him any more questions.

Whose Son Is the Christ?

[35]While Jesus was teaching in the temple courts, he asked, "How is it that the teachers of the law say that the Christ[c] is the son of David? [36]David himself, speaking by the Holy Spirit, declared:

" 'The Lord said to my Lord:
"Sit at my right hand
until I put your enemies
under your feet." '[d]

[37]David himself calls him 'Lord.' How then can he be his son?"
The large crowd listened to him with delight.

[38]As he taught, Jesus said, "Watch out for the teachers of the law. They like to walk around in flowing robes and be greeted in the marketplaces, [39]and have the most important seats in the synagogues and the places of honor at banquets. [40]They devour widows' houses and for a show make lengthy prayers. Such men will be punished most severely."

The Widow's Offering

[41]Jesus sat down opposite the place where the offerings were put and watched the crowd putting their money into the temple treasury. Many rich people threw in large amounts. [42]But a poor widow came and put in two very small copper coins,[e] worth only a fraction of a penny.[f]

[43]Calling his disciples to him, Jesus said, "I tell you the truth, this poor widow has put more into the treasury than all the others. [44]They all gave out of their wealth; but she, out of her poverty, put in everything—all she had to live on."

REFLECT: 1. Why do you give to God's work? What do you give besides money? **2.** If it's the coin that you give to "Caesar," what do you give to God? What often prevents you from giving to God what is God's? **3.** Would the church do better than "Caesar" with our taxes? Why or why not? **4.** In the three possibilities of love relationships (with God, neighbors, and self), where are you the strongest? The weakest? What have you found that enables love to grow in each area?

[z]29 Or *the Lord our God is one Lord*   [a]30 Deut. 6:4,5   [b]31 Lev. 19:18
[c]35 Or *Messiah*   [d]36 Psalm 110:1   [e]42 Greek *two lepta*   [f]42 Greek *kodrantes*

Notes, continued

so as to cover all conceivable situations that might arise. Others, such as this man, sought to reduce all law to a few foundational principles. For example, the great Rabbi Hillel was asked by a proselyte to tell him the whole law while standing on one leg. Hillel replied: "What you yourself hate, do not do to your neighbor: This is the whole law, the rest is commentary."

12:29-31 By his reply, Jesus demonstrates what a great moral teacher he is. First, he combines loving God with loving others, linking what had been seen as two quite different impulses. Second, he makes the commandment positive ("Love your neighbor") rather than negative ("Do not hate your neighbor"), thus calling people to active benevolence rather than merely avoiding conflict. Third, he broadened the definition of "neighbor" from meaning "other Jews" (its meaning in the context of Lev 19:18) to meaning "all people" (see Lk 10:25-37). Fourth, he made proper self-love (as distinguished from pride) the gauge by which individuals can know if they are loving others (see also 8:34-35; 9:33-35; 10:29-31).

12:29 Hear, O Israel... The Shema (a prayer taken from Dt 6:4), recited by pious Jews each morning and evening.

12:30 Jesus quotes the OT (Dt 6:5). **love**. In Greek this is *agape*. It means an active, benevolent giving to others without expectation of reward. *Agape* is not based on emotion ("I do this because I feel warmly toward you"), friendship ("I do this because you are a friend"), or kinship ("I do this because we are related"). *Agape* is rooted in the experience of God's unconditional love (which frees up a person to love others) and the obedient response to that love ("love your neighbor"; see Mt 5:43-48). **heart**. The inner life; the center of personality; where God reveals himself to a person. **soul**. The seat of life itself; the personality or ego. **mind**. The organ of knowledge; the intellect. **strength**. The power of a living being; the total effort behind heart, soul, and mind.

12:35-37 The essence of the argument is that if David acknowledges the Messiah's lordship ("David himself calls him 'Lord'"), this means that the Messiah must be something more than simply a descendent. The Messiah is not only David's son, but David's Lord. In saying this, Mark hints once again (see 12:6) that Jesus is more than just the Messiah. They will soon discover that he is also the Son of God. (The Greek word translated "Lord" was used in the Greek

OT as a name for God.) Furthermore, the Messiah's kingdom will be more than merely an earthly kingdom. The Psalm which Jesus quotes implies that the kingdom will be heavenly—the Messiah will not simply reestablish the Davidic kingdom. He will bring a new kingdom into being—one that will involve all peoples, not just the Jews. See the expanded discussion of Psalm 110:1 (which Jesus quotes) in Acts 2:29-36; 13:23-24 and Hebrews 1:5-13.

12:35 the Christ. This is the Greek word for Messiah: the expected deliverer of Israel (see notes on 8:27-9:1).

12:37 How then can he be his son? Jesus' listeners would have been unclear about the answer to this question. But Mark's readers know that Jesus, the Messiah, was indeed David's Lord.

12:38-40 At the start of this section, Jesus condemned the priests for their desecration of the temple (11:15-18). Here at the end of the section, he condemns the teachers of the law for using their position for personal aggrandizement, and not for service.

12:38 flowing robes. Long, white linen garments fringed with tassels that touched the ground. In such a stately garment, a person could not run or work and would be reckoned to be a person of leisure and importance. **greeted**. People considered the teachers of the law to be men of great insight and authority, and so they rose when they passed by and called out titles of respect.

12:39 the most important seats in the synagogue. The choice seat was up front, with its back to the box which contained the sacred Scriptures, and its front facing the congregation so that all would see who sat there.

12:40 They devour widows' houses. Since the teachers of the law were forbidden to receive pay for their teaching, they lived off others, including poor widows who were little able to support them.

12:41 temple treasury. This was located in the Court of Woman (the first of the inner courts of the temple). It consisted of 13 trumpet-shaped receptacles used to collect donations for the temple.

12:42 small copper coins. The smallest coins in circulation, worth 1/400 shekel, or about 1/8 of a cent.

UNIT 22 Signs of the End of the Age/Day and Hour Unknown

Mark 13:1-37

Signs of the End of the Age

13 As he was leaving the temple, one of his disciples said to him, "Look, Teacher! What massive stones! What magnificent buildings!"

²"Do you see all these great buildings?" replied Jesus. "Not one stone here will be left on another; every one will be thrown down."

³As Jesus was sitting on the Mount of Olives opposite the temple, Peter, James, John and Andrew asked him privately, ⁴"Tell us, when will these things happen? And what will be the sign that they are all about to be fulfilled?"

⁵Jesus said to them: "Watch out that no one deceives you. ⁶Many will come in my name, claiming, 'I am he,' and will deceive many. ⁷When you hear of wars and rumors of wars, do not be alarmed. Such things must happen, but the end is still to come. ⁸Nation will rise against nation, and kingdom against kingdom. There will be earthquakes in various places, and famines. These are the beginning of birth pains.

⁹"You must be on your guard. You will be handed over to the local councils and flogged in the synagogues. On account of me you will stand before governors and kings as witnesses to them. ¹⁰And the gospel must first be preached to all nations. ¹¹Whenever you are arrested and brought to trial, do not worry beforehand about what to say. Just say whatever is given you at the time, for it is not you speaking, but the Holy Spirit.

¹²"Brother will betray brother to death, and a father his child. Children will rebel against their parents and have them put to death. ¹³All men will hate you because of me, but he who stands firm to the end will be saved.

¹⁴"When you see 'the abomination that causes desolation'ᵍ standing where itʰ does not belong—let the reader understand—then let those who are in Judea flee to the mountains. ¹⁵Let no one on the roof of his house go down or enter the house to take anything out. ¹⁶Let no one in the field go back to get his cloak. ¹⁷How dreadful it will be in those days for pregnant women and nursing mothers! ¹⁸Pray that this will not take place in winter, ¹⁹because those will be days of distress unequaled from the beginning, when God created the world, until now—and never to be equaled again. ²⁰If the Lord had not cut short those days, no one would survive. But for the sake of the elect, whom he has chosen, he has shortened them. ²¹At that time if anyone says to you, 'Look, here is the Christⁱ!' or, 'Look, there he is!' do not believe it. ²²For false Christs and false prophets will appear

Questions

OPEN: 1. If you could take two things with you to heaven, what would they be? **2.** When in school or at work, have you "gotten burned" because you stood by the truth or refused to go along with the crowd? Was it worth it? Why or why not? **3.** Who pulled off the best surprise party on you? When?

DIG: 1. Why do you think that Jesus used the discussion about the temple to begin his discourse about the end of the age? What made the temple so significant for the disciples (see notes)? What would its destruction symbolize for them? **2.** Upon hearing this bombshell, what two questions do the disciples ask (v.4)? What events might deceive them into thinking the end times had come (vv.5-8)? Of what will these events be a sign? **3.** After that, what things will happen to the disciples and the church (vv.9-13; see notes on what happened to the early church in Acts)? To governors, kings, and "all nations"? What comfort and advocate will aid them to endure their trials? **4.** What dreadful event (v.14; see Da 9:26; 11:31; 12:11) will bring "days of distress" unequalled in human history? What deceptive signs will accompany that distress (vv.21-22)? **5.** How will the Son of Man come (vv.24-27)? **6.** How does the "fig tree" lesson (vv.28-29) answer the disciples' questions from verse 4 (see 11:12-14, 20-21)? To what do "these things" refer? Why do you think so? **7.** What promises does Jesus give in verses 30-31? How would this comfort (or discomfort) the disciples? What impact do these promises have on you, 20 centuries later? **8.** What visions in the past, present, and future do you see in these various *signs*: (a) "Wars and rumors of wars"? (b) Earthquakes and famines? (c) Trials and persecutions? (d) Family divisions? (e) World-wide evangelization? (f) False Christs and false prophets? **9.** Why do you think the Father has kept the time secret (v.32)? What is the responsibility of believers in the meantime?

[Scripture and questions continued on page 76]

ᵍ*14* Daniel 9:27; 11:31; 12:11   ʰ*14* Or *he;* also in verse 29   ⁱ*21* Or *Messiah*

Notes

13:1-37 This section contains the longest uninterrupted statement by Jesus in Mark's Gospel. It summarizes 11:1-12:44. The temple was the site and sometimes the subject of that section. Here Jesus predicts what will happen to the temple, and points out what lies ahead for his disciples. This is a very difficult section of Mark for modern readers to grasp, because it assumes a knowledge of Jewish ideas, aspirations, and history. In particular, it draws upon the concept of "The Day of the Lord" found in many OT writings (e.g., Isa 13:6-16; Joel 2-3; Am 5:16-20).

13:1-2 Jesus begins his discourse with a prediction that the temple will be destroyed (an event that will take place nearly 40 years later in A.D. 70). **What magnificent buildings!** The temple was a wonder to behold. It was built with huge white stones, some measuring 37 feet long by 12 feet high by 18 feet wide. Josephus described the temple: "The outward face. . .was covered all over with plates of gold of great weight, and, at the first rising of the sun, reflected back a very fiery splendor. . .The temple appeared to strangers when they were at a distance, like a mountain covered with snow. . ." **not one stone here will be left on another**. Josephus wrote: "Caesar (Titus) ordered the whole city and the temple to be razed to the ground." His orders were, indeed, carried out.

13:3-4 The disciples again come to Jesus, asking him to explain his teaching. To them, an event as cataclysmic as the temple's destruction must indicate the new age is coming (see Mt 24:3). **Mount of Olives**. A 2,700 foot mountain east of Jerusalem, it rose 200 feet higher than Mount Zion and afforded a magnificent view of the temple. **what will be the sign**. The question assumes that an omen will announce that the end of the world is at hand.

13:5-37 Jesus answers their question (in vv.28-31) after he lays a careful foundation. In his reply, he discusses three events: the suffering before the fall of Jerusalem (vv.5-13), the fall of Jerusalem (vv.14-23, 28-31) and the Second Coming (vv.24-27, 32-37).

13:5 This is a key theme in this section (see also vv.21-23, 33-37): vigilance against being deceived by those who claim that the end times have begun, or claim that they are prophets.

13:6-8 Various events will occur prior to the end: false prophets will come (v.6); there will be wars, earthquakes, and famine (vv.7-8). **'I am he.'** A claim by the false prophet to be the Messiah, or to be Jesus come again. Perhaps it will be a claim to deity, since this phrase was used in the OT for the name of God (see note on 6:50). **the end**. The end of the age or the end of the world—that time which precedes the full and open establishment of the kingdom of God. **is still to come**. Jesus does not say that the end will come immediately after these events, only that this is the "beginning of birth pains" (v.8), i.e., they signal that something is coming.

13:9-13 The focus shifts from the woes experienced by the whole world to the woes Christians will have to face. Specifically, they will be arrested and brought to trial. As Acts indicates, this happened to the early church (see Ac 4:1-23; 5:17-42; 6:8-7:60; 16:19-40; 22:30-23:10; 24:1-27; 25:1-12). They will be persecuted by both the Jews and the Gentiles (v.9) and by their own relatives (v.13). It will seem as if everyone is against them (v.13). Mark's readers were experiencing this, and so they would take comfort in the fact that such persecution was predicted by their Lord.

13:9 councils/synagogue. The councils are Jewish courts, where heretics were tried and then beaten publicly in the synagogue.

13:10 Despite the persecution, their mission will be to preach the gospel to all nations.

13:11 When they stand before their accusers, the Holy Spirit will give them the words of witness.

13:14-23 Having described what will precede the fall of Jerusalem, Jesus next turns to the event itself. When "the abomination that causes desolation" takes place, this will signal that the dark days have begun.

13:14 'the abomination that causes desolation.' This phrase is taken from the book of Daniel (see 9:27; 11:31; 12:11). It refers to an event so awful that Jews will flee from the temple in horror—such as in 168 B.C. when Antiochus Epiphanes, a Syrian king, captured Jerusalem. He set up an altar to Zeus in the temple and sacrificed a pig there. He also put public brothels in the temple courts. Jesus warns that when such an event occurs again, the fall of Jerusalem is imminent (see 2Th 2:1-4). **let those who are in Judea flee**. They must not seek safety in Jerusalem. Tradition has it that Christians fled Jerusalem prior to the siege by Titus in 70 A.D.

[Notes continued on page 77]

and perform signs and miracles to deceive the elect—if that were possible. ²³So be on your guard; I have told you everything ahead of time.

²⁴"But in those days, following that distress,

" 'the sun will be darkened,
   and the moon will not give its light;
²⁵the stars will fall from the sky,
   and the heavenly bodies will be shaken.'ʲ

²⁶"At that time men will see the Son of Man coming in clouds with great power and glory. ²⁷And he will send his angels and gather his elect from the four winds, from the ends of the earth to the ends of the heavens.

²⁸"Now learn this lesson from the fig tree: As soon as its twigs get tender and its leaves come out, you know that summer is near. ²⁹Even so, when you see these things happening, you know that it is near, right at the door. ³⁰I tell you the truth, this generationᵏ will certainly not pass away until all these things have happened. ³¹Heaven and earth will pass away, but my words will never pass away.

The Day and Hour Unknown

³²"No one knows about that day or hour, not even the angels in heaven, nor the Son, but only the Father. ³³Be on guard! Be alertˡ! You do not know when that time will come. ³⁴It's like a man going away: He leaves his house and puts his servants in charge, each with his assigned task, and tells the one at the door to keep watch.

³⁵"Therefore keep watch because you do not know when the owner of the house will come back—whether in the evening, or at midnight, or when the rooster crows, or at dawn. ³⁶If he comes suddenly, do not let him find you sleeping. ³⁷What I say to you, I say to everyone: 'Watch!' "

REFLECT: **1.** When you see the forces of evil apparently winning, do you feel like withdrawing from the battle and perching on the rooftop? Or rolling up your sleeves and getting into the fray? How does this passage encourage you? **2.** What is the most exciting thing to you about the Second Coming? The most distressing? What questions would you like to ask Jesus about it? **3.** Specifically, how can you fulfill verses 34 and 37: "Be on guard! Be alert... Watch!"?

ʲ25 Isaiah 13:10; 34:4   ᵏ30 Or *race*   ˡ33 Some manuscripts *alert and pray*

Notes, continued

13:15-16 *roof of his house*. The flat roof was used for midday prayer. It will be so urgent to flee that there will not even be time to go back into the house to pick up anything to take along. ***cloak***. The outer garment used as a blanket at night but taken off and left when working in the field during the day.

13:17-18 This will be a hard time, especially for women who are expecting or who have infants. It will be unfortunate if this takes place in winter when heavy rains swell the streams, making travel a problem.

13:19-20 The destruction of Jerusalem will be a disaster without parallel. Survival is made possible only by the mercy of God. ***the elect***. Whereas judgment has come upon Jerusalem and the temple, mercy is shown to the elect. The implied contrast is between the old order which is being swept away (symbolized by the temple), and the new order which is coming into being (the kingdom of God).

13:21-23 Still it is not yet the end time, Jesus warns. ***I have told you everything ahead of time***. Jesus' words of warning proved to be highly accurate. When the Jewish revolt broke out, the Romans moved in quickly to crush all resistance. Some Jews fled into Jerusalem for safety and were trapped there (see v.14). During the siege several leaders arose, each claiming that God had sent him to save the city.

13:24-27 Jesus now describes the second coming of the Son of Man in power and glory. The destruction of Jerusalem is the result of human failure and evil. It will bring suffering and hardship. The Second Coming, on the other hand, will bring salvation and blessing to the people of God.

12:24-25 In the OT, such events were seen as a sign of God's judgment (see Eze 32:7-8; Joel 2:10-11; Am 8:9-10). ***in those days***. No time frame is specified in this phrase. Jesus says that the Second Coming will take place sometime after the fall of Jerusalem.

13:26 *the Son of Man*. Here Jesus clearly reveals the nature of the Son of Man: he is a divine being who will draw history to a close (see note on 2:28). ***coming in clouds with great power and glory***. In the OT, God is described with phrases like this (e.g. Ex 19:9, 34:5; Ps 104:3; Isa 19:1).

13:27 *gather his elect*. It is God who will do this (see Dt 30:3-4; Ps 50:3-5; Isa 43:5-6). In verses 26-27,

Jesus makes it quite clear who he is: the Son of God (see note on 12:6).

13:28-37 With all this as background (vv.5-27), Jesus can now respond to the disciples' original question (v.4). His response is that one event (the fall of Jerusalem) will occur within their lifetimes, but they are not to be deceived. This will not usher in the end time. Jesus encourages the disciples to be vigilant, but not to worry about when all this will take place.

13:28 *lesson from the fig tree*. They knew that the fig tree only got its leaves in late spring. When the leaves come it is a sure sign that summer was near. This is a reference to the rather mysterious cursing of the fig tree by Jesus in 11:12-14, 20-21 (see notes there), and has to do with the judgment on Jerusalem.

13:29 *these things*. Jesus uses the phrase "these things" (vv.4,8)—the signs to which the disciples must be alert are those that will occur in their lifetime, namely the fall of Jerusalem, which is described in verses 5-23. The phrase "these things" cannot refer to verses 24-27, since those verses describe the end itself and not the events preceding the end.

13:30 Jesus makes quite clear in this verse that he has in mind the near event when he refers to the lesson of the fig tree (the fall of Jerusalem), and not the distant event (the Second Coming).

13:32-37 Now Jesus refers to the Second Coming. Only God knows when this event will occur. The role of the disciples in this case is not to read the signs (as with the fall of Jerusalem), but to be ready (since it can occur at any moment).

13:32 *that day*. The end of time when God rescues his people and makes manifest his kingdom (see Joel 3:18; Am 8:3,9,13; 9:11; Mic 4:6; 5:10; 7:11-12; Zep 1:9-10; 3:11,16; Zec 9:16).

13:34-36 Jesus uses an example. When the master is away, his servants are to attend to their duties. They are not to sleep (in contrast to "watching"). "The work that the servants are to do is of course not primarily scanning the horizon for the master's return and then rushing about in a dither but rather the steady, regular performance of their tasks" (Hurtado).

13:37 It is not just the Twelve who must get on with the mission of God when Jesus is gone. It is everyone:

UNIT 23 Jesus Anointed at Bethany/The Lord's Supper/Jesus Predicts Peter's Denial

Mark 14:1-31

Jesus Anointed at Bethany

14 Now the Passover and the Feast of Unleavened Bread were only two days away, and the chief priests and the teachers of the law were looking for some sly way to arrest Jesus and kill him. ²"But not during the Feast," they said, "or the people may riot."

³While he was in Bethany, reclining at the table in the home of a man known as Simon the Leper, a woman came with an alabaster jar of very expensive perfume, made of pure nard. She broke the jar and poured the perfume on his head.

⁴Some of those present were saying indignantly to one another, "Why this waste of perfume? ⁵It could have been sold for more than a year's wages ⁿand the money given to the poor." And they rebuked her harshly.

⁶"Leave her alone," said Jesus. "Why are you bothering her? She has done a beautiful thing to me. ⁷The poor you will always have with you, and you can help them any time you want. But you will not always have me. ⁸She did what she could. She poured perfume on my body beforehand to prepare for my burial. ⁹I tell you the truth, wherever the gospel is preached throughout the world, what she has done will also be told, in memory of her."

¹⁰Then Judas Iscariot, one of the Twelve, went to the chief priests to betray Jesus to them. ¹¹They were delighted to hear this and promised to give him money. So he watched for an opportunity to hand him over.

The Lord's Supper

¹²On the first day of the Feast of Unleavened Bread, when it was customary to sacrifice the Passover lamb, Jesus' disciples asked him, "Where do you want us to go and make preparations for you to eat the Passover?"

¹³So he sent two of his disciples, telling them, "Go into the city, and a man carrying a jar of water will meet you. Follow him. ¹⁴Say to the owner of the house he enters, 'The Teacher asks: Where is my guest room, where I may eat the Passover with my disciples?' ¹⁵He will show you a large upper room, furnished and ready. Make preparations for us there."

Questions

OPEN: 1. If you had a year's salary to blow on friends, which would you choose: (a) Big party for all, (b) Glorious trip for a few, or (c) Extravagant gift for one? **2.** What one gift you received stands out in your memory? Why?

DIG: 1. What was significant about this time of year? How might this cause the fear expressed by Jesus' opponents? **2.** How does this woman's action (v.3) strike you: Thoughtful, but misguided? Tasteful, but extravagant? Wasteful, no buts about it? Honoring to the nth degree? **3.** Do you think the perfume could have been better spent? Why? How was her action justified by Jesus (vv.6-9) and used by Judas (vv.10-11)? **4.** In verses 12-26, how does this meal relate to the Passover (see Ex 12)? **5.** What preparations are involved (see notes)? Why would secrecy be needed as this meal was planned? What risk was involved? **6.** What does Jesus say about his betrayer? How do the disciples react to that bombshell? **7.** What new meaning does Jesus give to the Passover bread? The wine? What related vow does he make? **8.** How much do you think the disciples understood when Jesus spoke about his body and blood? What clue to the meaning of Jesus' death and resurrection would later be provided by reference to the first Passover (see Ex 12)? **9.** Were the disciples singing their last hymn together (v.26) in a minor or major key? Why do you think so? **10.** In verses 27-31, how does Peter see himself in relation to the other disciples? How might the others feel about that? **11.** Why do you think Jesus warned the disciples (especially Peter) of their upcoming denial?

[Scripture and questions continued on page 80]

ⁿ5 Greek *than three hundred denarii*

Notes

14:1-16:8 Jesus has warned his disciples a number of times about what lies ahead for him: rejection by the religious leaders, suffering, death, and then resurrection. In the final chapters of his Gospel, Mark describes these events as they unfold. They will reveal that Jesus is not just the Messiah; he is also the Son of God.

14:1 *The Passover*. A feast in which the people of Israel celebrated God's deliverance of their nation from Egypt where they had been held as slaves (see Ex 12). On this particular Passover, God would once again rescue his people, though in a totally unexpected way—namely through the death of his own Son. ***the Feast of Unleavened Bread***. By the time of the first century, this feast was coupled with the Passover so that there was a week of feasting. ***some sly way to arrest Jesus and kill him***. The religious leadership had already decided to kill Jesus (see 3:6; 12:12). Now they are seeking a way to do so.

14:2 During Passover, Jerusalem's population rose from 50,000 to 250,000, making the potential for rioting against Rome great, as this huge mob of pilgrims remembered together (in the Passover ritual) past oppression by a foreign power. The Jewish officials could not afford to spark a riot by arresting Jesus, lest they incur harsh Roman repression.

14:3 *reclining*. Banquets were generally eaten lying on a low couch or pillows. ***a woman came***. A woman would not be present at a meal like this except to serve. Her entrance would have been scandalous. ***perfume***. Nard was a much-prized aromatic oil extracted from an Indian root. It was stored in long-necked alabaster flasks to retain its aroma. The neck was broken off when the perfume was used. Possibly this was a family heirloom.

14:4-5 *the money given to the poor*. The indignation of the disciples (see Mt 26:8) is understandable. It was the custom at the Passover to remember the poor with gifts. (Of course, Jesus is himself one of the poor, making the gift to him appropriate.)

14:7 Jesus quotes from Deuteronomy 15:11, pointing out that what is about to happen to him is unique.

14:8 It is not clear whether this woman knows that Jesus will die shortly. (This fact has repeatedly eluded the disciples, despite Jesus' teaching that he would—see 8:31-33; 9:32; 10:35-38.) This was probably an act of love on the part of one of his followers. Jesus, however, interprets her gift as a preparation for this death. ***to prepare for my burial***. The bodies of the dead were anointed with oil. However, Jesus would die as a criminal and so would not have been anointed had it not been for this woman.

14:9 As Jesus' words indicate, this is another acted-out parable like the cursing of the fig tree (see note on 11:14). ***what she has done will also be told***. The inclusion of this story in three of the Gospels (see Mt 26:6-13 and Jn 12:1-8) is a fulfillment of Jesus' prophecy.

14:10-11 In contrast to the single-minded devotion of this woman stands the act of treachery on the part of Judas. Mark gives no reasons for his betrayal. Matthew mentions the money he received (Mt 26:15), while Luke and John say that he was impelled by Satan (Lk 22:3; Jn 13:2,27). Judas offers the officials a way to arrest Jesus without the public knowing it. He will tell them when and where Jesus will be alone (see vv.1-2).

14:12 *sacrifice the Passover lamb*. Each pilgrim sacrificed his own lamb in the temple. A priest caught the blood in a bowl and this was thrown on the altar. After removing certain parts of the lamb for sacrifice, the carcass was returned to the pilgrim to be roasted and eaten for Passover. Josephus estimated that one-quarter million lambs were killed at Passover, turning the temple courts into a bloody mess. ***make preparations***. The disciples have to set out the unleavened bread and the wine (which was mixed with water); collect the bitter herbs (horseradish, chicory, etc.); make the sauce in which the bread was dipped (a stew of dried fruit, spices, and wine); and roast the lamb on an open fire. ***eat the Passover***. The meal began with a blessing and the first (of four) cups of wine. Psalms were then sung and the story of the Deliverance read, followed by the second cup of wine and the eating of the bread, herbs, and the sauce (into which Judas and the others dip their bread—see v.20). Then the meal of roast lamb and bread is eaten. More prayers are said and the third cup is drunk. More Psalms are sung; the final cup is drunk, after which a Psalm is sung. Two short prayers end the feast.

[Notes continued on page 81]

Mark 14:1-31, continued

¹⁶The disciples left, went into the city and found things just as Jesus had told them. So they prepared the Passover.

¹⁷When evening came, Jesus arrived with the Twelve. ¹⁸While they were reclining at the table eating, he said, "I tell you the truth, one of you will betray me—one who is eating with me."

¹⁹They were saddened, and one by one they said to him, "Surely not I?"

²⁰"It is one of the Twelve," he replied, "one who dips bread into the bowl with me. ²¹The Son of Man will go just as it is written about him. But woe to that man who betrays the Son of Man! It would be better for him if he had not been born."

²²While they were eating, Jesus took bread, gave thanks and broke it, and gave it to his disciples, saying, "Take it; this is my body."

²³Then he took the cup, gave thanks and offered it to them, and they all drank from it.

²⁴"This is my blood of theⁿ covenant, which is poured out for many," he said to them. ²⁵"I tell you the truth, I will not drink again of the fruit of the vine until that day when I drink it anew in the kingdom of God."

²⁶When they had sung a hymn, they went out to the Mount of Olives.

Jesus Predicts Peter's Denial

²⁷"You will all fall away," Jesus told them, "for it is written:

" 'I will strike the shepherd,
and the sheep will be scattered.'^o

²⁸But after I have risen, I will go ahead of you into Galilee."

²⁹Peter declared, "Even if all fall away, I will not."

³⁰"I tell you the truth," Jesus answered, "today—yes, tonight—before the rooster crows twice^p you yourself will disown me three times."

³¹But Peter insisted emphatically, "Even if I have to die with you, I will never disown you." And all the others said the same.

REFLECT: 1. What "beautiful thing" (v.6) would you like to do for Jesus that others might see as being very wasteful? **2.** How would you have felt if you had been at that meal (vv.12-20)? How would you have felt if you had known about the things to come: Would you then try to stop either the betrayer or Jesus? Why or why not? **3.** What is your focus when you partake of Communion? Why is Communion important to the body of believers?

ⁿ24 Some manuscripts *the new*   ^o27 Zech. 13:7   ^p30 Some early manuscripts do not have *twice.*

Notes, continued

14:13-16 Instructions for Jesus' arrest had already been issued (see Jn 11:57). He knew that the officials were looking for him in places away from the crowd. To guard against being arrested at night, he would generally sleep in Bethany, which was outside the jurisdiction of the priests. But the law required that he eat the Passover meal in Jerusalem itself, hence the need for secret arrangements. The irony is that Jesus knows full well that he will be betrayed from within his own circle of disciples (see vv.18-21; 27-31). Jesus' instructions here parallel those he gave concerning the donkey on which he first rode into the city (see 11:1-6). It is clear that he had been to Jerusalem previously, at which time he made these arrangements. It is also clear that he is arranging the events so that they happen in such a way as to reveal who he is.

14:13 *a man carrying a jar of water*. Such a person would have been easy to spot and follow, since it was highly unusual for a man to carry a jug. Women carried jugs; men carried wineskins.

14:17 *When evening came*. The Passover meal could be eaten only after sunset. It was a night of excited watching in which people asked: "Will this be the night when God comes again to deliver his people from bondage?"

14:18-21 Jesus predicts that one of his disciples will betray him.

14:21 *as it is written about him*. Passages such as Isaiah 53:1-6 point to the suffering of God's chosen servant.

14:22 To share in the torn Passover bread, which Jesus reinterprets as his own person, is to share in his life, mission, and destiny.

14:22-26 Jesus' celebration of the Last Supper provides the model for how the Church came to celebrate Communion (see 1Co 11:23-26). His use of the bread and the cup in a symbolic way was consistent with the way in which the various elements of the Passover meal were used symbolically (e.g., the bowl of salt water was used to remind them of the tears shed in Egypt, and of the Red Sea through which they passed). The symbols in the Passover meal pointed back to the first covenant God made with Israel, while Jesus' words here at the Last Supper pointed forward to his death and the new covenant which would result from it.

14:23 *cup*. Jesus relates the Passover cup of red wine to the renewal of the covenant of God with his people via his sacrificial death. ***gave thanks***. The Greek word "to give thanks" is *eucharisto*, from which the English word Eucharist is derived.

14:24 *covenant*. In general terms, this is a treaty between two parties. Such an agreement was often sealed by the sacrifice of an animal. In specific terms, it refers to the arrangement that God made with Israel (see Ex 24:1-8) which was dependent on Israel's obedience. Now (as anticipated in Jer 31:31-33) a new covenant is established, which is made dependent on Jesus' obedience (his sacrificial death). A covenant of law becomes a covenant of love. ***poured out***. Blood which was poured out symbolized a violent death (see Ge 4:10-11; Dt 19:10; Mt 23:35). This phrase points to the type of the death Jesus would have. ***for many***. See 10:45.

14:25 Jesus abstains from the fourth Passover cup.

14:26 The Hallel (Ps 113-118) was sung at the Passover; the first part (Ps 113-114) prior to the meal and the second part, mentioned here, after the meal (Ps 115-118).

14:27-31 Jesus predicts that not only will Judas betray him, but so too will the others! Peter protests strongly that he will not betray Jesus, but events show that he (as well as the others) does this very thing (see 14:50, 66-72). This betrayal is the experience that reveals to the disciples the tentativeness and self-interest that characterizes their pre-resurrection faith.

14:28 Not only does he predict their falling away, he also anticipates their rejoining him after his resurrection (see 16:7).

14:31 *I will not*. This is a very strong negative meaning "I will by no means." It is inconceivable to Peter that he would desert Jesus.

UNIT 24 Gethsemane/Jesus Arrested/Before the Sanhedrin/Peter Disowns Jesus

Mark 14:32-72

Questions

Gethsemane

³²They went to a place called Gethsemane, and Jesus said to his disciples, "Sit here while I pray." ³³He took Peter, James and John along with him, and he began to be deeply distressed and troubled. ³⁴"My soul is overwhelmed with sorrow to the point of death," he said to them. "Stay here and keep watch."

³⁵Going a little farther, he fell to the ground and prayed that if possible the hour might pass from him. ³⁶"*Abba,*ᵠ Father," he said, "everything is possible for you. Take this cup from me. Yet not what I will, but what you will."

³⁷Then he returned to his disciples and found them sleeping. "Simon," he said to Peter, "are you asleep? Could you not keep watch for one hour? ³⁸Watch and pray so that you will not fall into temptation. The spirit is willing, but the body is weak."

³⁹Once more he went away and prayed the same thing. ⁴⁰When he came back, he again found them sleeping, because their eyes were heavy. They did not know what to say to him.

⁴¹Returning the third time, he said to them, "Are you still sleeping and resting? Enough! The hour has come. Look, the Son of Man is betrayed into the hands of sinners. ⁴²Rise! Let us go! Here comes my betrayer!"

Jesus Arrested

⁴³Just as he was speaking, Judas, one of the Twelve, appeared. With him was a crowd armed with swords and clubs, sent from the chief priests, the teachers of the law, and the elders. ⁴⁴Now the betrayer had arranged a signal with them: "The one I kiss is the man; arrest him and lead him away under guard." ⁴⁵Going at once to Jesus, Judas said, "Rabbi!" and kissed him. ⁴⁶The men seized Jesus and arrested him. ⁴⁷Then one of those standing near drew his sword and struck the servant of the high priest, cutting off his ear.

⁴⁸"Am I leading a rebellion," said Jesus, "that you have come out with swords and clubs to capture me? ⁴⁹Every day I was with you, teaching in the temple courts, and you did not arrest me. But the Scriptures must be fulfilled." ⁵⁰Then everyone deserted him and fled.

⁵¹A young man, wearing nothing but a linen garment, was following Jesus. When they seized him, ⁵²he fled naked, leaving his garment behind.

OPEN: Where do you go (or what do you do) when you're facing difficult dituations? Do you prefer to be alone at these times, or in the company of close friends?

DIG: 1. Why did Jesus take Peter, James, and John with him to pray (v.33)? **2.** Why don't the disciples share Jesus' sense of urgency? How does this relate to their statements in the previous passage? **3.** What did Jesus desire most of all? Yet how did he pray? Why? **4.** Why did Jesus urge Peter specifically to "watch and pray"? **5.** What irony do you see here? **6.** From this story, what key thing do you learn about Jesus? About human weakness and failure? About affirming God's will? **7.** Why is the crowd armed (vv. 43,48)? What does this tell you about Judas' misunderstanding of Jesus' mission? **8.** What Scriptures were fulfilled (see notes)? **9.** How do you account for the disciples' reactions (vv.47,50,51)? **10.** What empathy (if any) do you have for Judas? How do you think he felt toward Jesus? Why do you think he did what he did? **11.**

[Scripture and questions continued on page 84]

ᵠ36 Aramaic for *Father*

Notes

14:32-42 Two themes dominate this section: Jesus' continued obedience to God despite his dread of what was coming, and the disciples' continued failure to grasp what lay ahead for Jesus.

14:32 Gethsemane. An olive orchard in an estate at the foot of the Mount of Olives just outside the eastern wall of Jerusalem. The name means lit., "an oil press" (for making olive oil).

14:33 Peter, James and John. Once again, these three men accompany Jesus during a time of great significance. Interestingly, neither the rebuke of Peter (8:32) nor the self-centered request of James and John (10:35-40) has damaged their relationship with Jesus. Also note that each of these men has vowed to stay with Jesus through thick or thin (see 10:38-39; 14:29,31). What Jesus asks them to share with him is not glory (which they wanted), but sorrow (which they kept denying would come). **deeply distressed**. Lit., filled with "shuddering awe." Jesus is filled with deep sorrow as the impact of submitting to God's will hits him.

14:35 He would have prayed aloud, as was his custom, so the disciples heard (and remembered) his prayer. This is the third time in Mark that Jesus has been shown at prayer (see also 1:35; 6:46).

14:36 Abba. This is how a child would address his father: "Daddy." This was not a title that was used in prayer in the first century. **this cup**. By this image, Jesus refers to the events of his death that are fast coming on him (see also 10:38-39).

14:37 sleeping. It was very late (the Passover could extend up to midnight), and they had drunk at least four cups of wine.

14:38 To "watch" means to "be spiritually alert," lest they fall into the "temptation" to be unfaithful to God (see also 13:37). The "flesh" (i.e., "inadequate human resources") will fail them despite the willingness of God's "spirit." To the very end, even the three disciples most intimately connected with Jesus fail to understand his teaching about what it means to be the Messiah. Had they done so, they would have prepared themselves for the danger that lay ahead. They would also have helped Jesus as he prepared for the impending crisis. As it is, Jesus is all alone in his sorrow. **temptation**. The trial or test that is about to come upon them.

14:41 into the hands of sinners. This refers to the religious authorities that Jesus confronted in the previous unit (11:1-13:37) who have corrupted the offices they hold. The irony of this assessment is that the term "sinners" was used by these religious leaders to refer to others: to Jews who did not live by the law, and to all Gentiles. In fact, it is a term they have earned by their actions.

14:43 a crowd. The Sanhedrin commanded the services of the Temple Police (who were Levites) and of an auxiliary police force (servants of the court) who maintained order outside the temple area. **the chief priests, the teachers of the law, and the elders**. See 8:31.

14:44 a kiss. This was a normal form of greeting. However, the intensive form of verb used here indicates that Judas' actual kiss was a warm and affectionate greeting and not merely perfunctory.

14:45 Rabbi! This title was a form of respect. It meant lit., "My Great One." By his greeting, by his kiss, and by sharing the same bowl (v.20—to eat together was a sign of friendship), Judas conveys the sense of a warm relationship with Jesus.

14:46 arrested him. The charge is not given. Perhaps it was blasphemy (2:7), violation of the Sabbath (2:24; 3:2-6), or the practice of magic (3:22).

14:47 one of those standing near. According to John's Gospel (18:10), this was Peter. **drew his sword**. That Peter should have a sword is not unusual. Travellers carried them as protection against robbers and the disciples have just completed a journey from Jerusalem to Galilee (see Lk 22:36-38).

14:48 What Jesus is saying is saying here is that he is not a bandit nor a guerrilla leading a resistance movement, so why have they come armed to arrest him?

14:49 the Scriptures. Jesus is probably referring to Zechariah 13:7 (see also Mk 14:27), but he may also have in mind Isaiah 53:12 and Psalm 41:9.

14:51-52 a young man. It has been suggested that this is Mark himself. He lived in Jerusalem (Ac 12:12), and there is a tradition that the Last Supper

[Notes continued on page 85]   83

Mark 14:32-72, continued

Questions

Before the Sanhedrin

⁵³They took Jesus to the high priest, and all the chief priests, elders and teachers of the law came together. ⁵⁴Peter followed him at a distance, right into the courtyard of the high priest. There he sat with the guards and warmed himself at the fire.

⁵⁵The chief priests and the whole Sanhedrin were looking for evidence against Jesus so that they could put him to death, but they did not find any. ⁵⁶Many testified falsely against him, but their statements did not agree.

⁵⁷Then some stood up and gave this false testimony against him: ⁵⁸"We heard him say, 'I will destroy this man-made temple and in three days will build another, not made by man.' " ⁵⁹Yet even then their testimony did not agree.

⁶⁰Then the high priest stood up before them and asked Jesus, "Are you not going to answer? What is this testimony that these men are bringing against you?" ⁶¹But Jesus remained silent and gave no answer.

Again the high priest asked him, "Are you the Christ,ʳ the Son of the Blessed One?"

⁶²"I am," said Jesus. "And you will see the Son of Man sitting at the right hand of the Mighty One and coming on the clouds of heaven."

⁶³The high priest tore his clothes. "Why do we need any more witnesses?" he asked. ⁶⁴"You have heard the blasphemy. What do you think?"

They all condemned him as worthy of death. ⁶⁵Then some began to spit at him; they blindfolded him, struck him with their fists, and said, "Prophesy!" And the guards took him and beat him.

What does the fact that Peter followed Jesus (but at a distance) tell you about Peter's character? **12.** What evidence do the chief priests initially seek against Jesus? Why do you think that Jesus, for the most part, remains silent? **13.** On what evidence is the final decision against Jesus based? Why would the chief priests see Jesus as a blasphemer? **14.** What is the significance of Jesus' messianic acknowledgement, the first direct confession recorded in Mark (v.62; see Ps 110:1 and Da 7: 13)? **15.** How seriously would a charge of blasphemy be taken by the Roman authorities (see 15:14)? How does this present a problem for the Jewish authorities? **16.** What perversion of justice do you see in this "trial"? **17.** Peter is brave enough to follow Jesus to the high priest's house. Why do you think he now denies Christ? Do you think he realized what he was doing? Why? **18.** How were the three denials similar? Different? **19.** In retrospect (see 14:29-31), how does Peter feel? **20.** Do you think the situation would have been different if Peter had heeded Jesus' command to "watch and pray" (14:38)? Why?

[Scripture and questions continued on page 86]

ʳ61 Or *Messiah*

Notes, continued

was held in the upper room of his mother's house. In that case, it is not inconceivable that Mark heard Jesus and the disciples leaving, got out of bed, threw a sheet around himself, and secretly followed after them. **linen garment**. Probably a bed sheet. The fact that it is linen means that he came from a wealthy family.

14:53-65 In the trial of Jesus, Mark shows how it is that a criminal could be the Messiah. (This was one of the impediments to belief among the Roman population.) As quickly becomes evident, Jesus was no criminal. No charge was laid against him (much less proved), except that he claimed to be the Messiah, which is exactly who he was. His "trial" was a perversion of justice.

14:53 the high priest. The spiritual head of Israel. Caiaphas was the high priest before whom Jesus came (Mt 26:57).

14:55 the whole Sanhedrin. A council consisting of seventy-one leaders, both priests and laymen, who made up the highest Jewish court. They were given authority by Rome to rule in matters of religious law. **evidence**. To convict someone of a capital crime required the unanimous testimony of at least two witnesses. Each witness gave his testimony individually to the judge in the presence of the accused. If two witnesses differed in their accounts (even in the smallest of details), their testimony was thrown out of court (see Dt 19:15).

14:58 Jesus did, in fact, say something like this (Jn 2:19), but what he meant is quite different from the way it is understood here. He was referring to his own bodily resurrection after three days (Jn 2:21). It was a capital offense to desecrate or destroy a place of worship.

14:59 Since the witnesses did not agree, this charge could not be used against Jesus.

14:61-62 These are key verses in the Gospel. The three titles which reveal who Jesus is are combined together here: Messiah, Son of God ("Son of the Blessed One"), and Son of Man. Jesus has referred to himself as the Son of Man, since up to this point had he used the other titles, they would have been misunderstood. Now it becomes clear that the Son of Man is the Messiah, who is the Son of God.

14:61 Since they could not produce evidence, their final recourse was this desperate attempt by Caiaphas to get Jesus to say he was the Messiah. If Jesus admitted to being the Messiah, it would be a clear case of blasphemy, since in their eyes it would be ludicrous that a person such as Jesus could be the Messiah (see 3:22-30). **the Blessed One**. Pious Jews would not refer directly to God by name. This phrase was one of a number used as a substitute for his name (see v.62).

14:62 This is the first time in Mark that Jesus openly and unequivocally declares his Messiahship. The time for secrecy is past. The verses Jesus quotes (a combination of Ps 110:1 and Da 7:13-14) simply reiterate, in biblical images, his claim of messiahship (see 8:38; 12:35-37; and 13:26, where these passages are also referred to). **I am**. This forthright declaration by Jesus of his identity (despite the consequences) was a powerful example for the Christians at Rome, who were also being called upon at that time to confess their faith before the authorities. This was also an allusion to the name of God (see 6:50). **sitting at the right hand**. To sit here was to sit in the place of honor (see 10:33). Jesus too, like the figure in Daniel 7, will be vindicated at the Second Coming, when all his accusers see that his claim was true.

14:63 tore his clothes. By tearing his clothes, Caiaphas signaled that he was profoundly disturbed by Jesus' statement (see 2Ki 19:1).

14:64 blasphemy. Dishonoring or slandering another. The penalty for blaspheming God was death by stoning (Lev 24:10-16). By claiming to be the Messiah, the Sanhedrin understood Jesus to be dishonoring God. In fact, it is they who are guilty of blasphemy by refusing to recognize who Jesus is. God himself has declared Jesus to be his son (see 1:11; 9:7). Jesus has already been charged with blasphemy several times for being who he is (see 2:7; 3:28). **worthy of death**. At that point in history, the Sanhedrin did not have the power to carry out a death sentence. Only the Roman procurator could do that.

14:65 In this way the council demonstrated that it was opposed to what Jesus had done. The blows and spitting were traditional ways of expressing abhorrence and repudiation (see Num 12;14; Dt 25:9; Job 30:10; Isa 50:6). **they blindfolded him**.

[Notes continued on page 87]

Mark 14:32-72, continued

Questions

Peter Disowns Jesus

⁶⁶While Peter was below in the courtyard, one of the servant girls of the high priest came by. ⁶⁷When she saw Peter warming himself, she looked closely at him.

"You also were with that Nazarene, Jesus," she said.

⁶⁸But he denied it. "I don't know or understand what you're talking about," he said, and went out into the entryway.ˢ

⁶⁹When the servant girl saw him there, she said again to those standing around, "This fellow is one of them." ⁷⁰Again he denied it.

After a little while, those standing near said to Peter, "Surely you are one of them, for you are a Galilean."

⁷¹He began to call down curses on himself, and he swore to them, "I don't know this man you're talking about."

⁷²Immediately the rooster crowed the second time.ᵗ Then Peter remembered the word Jesus had spoken to him: "Before the rooster crows twiceᵘ you will disown me three times." And he broke down and wept.

ˢ68 Some early manuscripts *entryway and the rooster crowed*   ᵗ7 2 Some early manuscripts do not have *the second time*.   ᵘ72 Some early manuscripts do not have *twice*.

86

Notes, continued

Isaiah 11:2-4 had been interpreted to mean that the Messiah could make judgments on the basis of smell alone without the aid of sight. **Prophesy!** They are asking him to prove his claim to be the Messiah by naming who it was that had struck him while he was blindfolded.

14:66-72 The account of Peter's betrayal (which began in v.54) is concluded here. The story of Peter's "trial" is set in contrast to the trial of Jesus. Jesus' forthright declaration of who he is before the high priest (v.62) is the opposite of Peter's denial of who he is before the servant girl (14:66-70a) and the stranger (14:70b-71).

14:71 *call down curses on himself*. Peter even goes so far as to call down on himself the wrath of God if he is not telling the truth (which he knows he is not)! ***I don't know this man***. This, like his previous denial (v.68), is an outright lie. ***this man you are talking about***. Peter does not use Jesus' name (see also 8:38).

14:72 *the rooster crowed the second time*. Roosters in Palestine crowed first at about 12:30 a.m., then again at about 1:30 a.m., and for a third time at about 2:30 a.m. As a result of this peculiar habit, the watch kept by soldiers in Palestine from midnight until 3:00 a.m. was called "cock-crow." Peter's denials were therefore spread over an hour. ***wept***. Peter suddenly realizes what he has done. Despite his vigorous assertion that he would never deny Jesus, this is exactly what he did. To make matters worse, he denied Jesus before rather unintimidating people (a servant girl and an anonymous man), and did so with a formal oath (v.68) and by curses (v.71). The crowing rooster reveals to him his sin, and he weeps tears of repentance.

UNIT 25 Jesus Before Pilate/Soldiers Mock Jesus/ Crucifixion/Death of Jesus

Mark 15:1-41

Questions

Jesus Before Pilate

15 Very early in the morning, the chief priests, with the elders, the teachers of the law and the whole Sanhedrin, reached a decision. They bound Jesus, led him away and handed him over to Pilate.

²"Are you the king of the Jews?" asked Pilate.

"Yes, it is as you say," Jesus replied.

³The chief priests accused him of many things. ⁴So again Pilate asked him, "Aren't you going to answer? See how many things they are accusing you of."

⁵But Jesus still made no reply, and Pilate was amazed.

⁶Now it was the custom at the Feast to release a prisoner whom the people requested. ⁷A man called Barabbas was in prison with the insurrectionists who had committed murder in the uprising. ⁸The crowd came up and asked Pilate to do for them what he usually did.

⁹"Do you want me to release to you the king of the Jews?" asked Pilate, ¹⁰knowing it was out of envy that the chief priests had handed Jesus over to him. ¹¹But the chief priests stirred up the crowd to have Pilate release Barabbas instead.

¹²"What shall I do, then, with the one you call the king of the Jews?" Pilate asked them.

¹³"Crucify him!" they shouted.

¹⁴"Why? What crime has he committed?" asked Pilate.

But they shouted all the louder, "Crucify him!"

¹⁵Wanting to satisfy the crowd, Pilate released Barabbas to them. He had Jesus flogged, and handed him over to be crucified.

The Soldiers Mock Jesus

¹⁶The soldiers led Jesus away into the palace (that is, the Praetorium) and called together the whole company of soldiers. ¹⁷They put a purple robe on him, then twisted together a crown of thorns and set it on him. ¹⁸And they began to call out to him, "Hail, king of the Jews!" ¹⁹Again and again they struck him on the head with a staff and spit on him. Falling on their knees, they paid homage to him. ²⁰And when they had mocked him, they took off the purple robe and put his own clothes on him. Then they led him out to crucify him.

[Scripture and questions continued on page 90]

OPEN: 1. As a kid, would you rather have been punished by Mom or Dad? Why? **2.** In grade school, were you the type to pick on others, or the type who was picked on? **3.** Have you ever sat with someone who was dying? What was it like?

DIG: 1. What insights into Pilate's and Jesus' character does this story offer? Why is Pilate indecisive? Why is Jesus silent? How do these character traits interact here? **2.** Why do the people (after witnessing Jesus' miracles, hearing his teachings, and praising him with hosannas) now demand that Jesus be crucified? **3.** Why does Pilate grant their request: Out of concern for justice? Peace-at-any-price? Spineless fence-straddling? **4.** What insights about the gospel do you see in the release of Barabbas in exchange for Jesus (see 8:37; 10:45)? **5.** What mental, physical, and emotional brutality do the soldiers inflict upon Jesus? Why? Does their mockery stem from fear, anger, unbelief, or what? **6.** Why is Simon needed to carry Jesus' cross (see 14:65; 15:15,19)? How might that affect him? **7.** What kinds of people were usually crucified (v.27)? How is Jesus like them? **8.** What further insults are added to injury (vv.29-32)? What prophecy does this fulfill? **9.** What ironies do you see here: In the places occupied by the robbers (see 10:37)? In the call for Jesus to save himself by coming down from the cross? In the officially posted reason for Jesus' death? **10.** What aspect of the crucifixion was the worst for Jesus: The physical pain? The spiritual separation from God? Why? What causes his separation from the Father (see Hab 1:13)? What does this say about our part in his crucifixion? **11.** How are the cry of Jesus (v.34; also Ps 22:1), the tearing of the temple curtain (v.38; see Heb 10:19ff.), and the faith of the centurion (v.39) all related? **12.** What do you learn about Joseph (vv.43-46)? What risks does a man of his status take by asking for the body of a condemned criminal?

Notes

15:1-20 The Jewish trial is now followed by a Roman trial. The Jewish high court consisted of the 71 members of the Sanhedrin; the Roman court involved only one man. The trial before the Sanhedrin was conducted secretly, out of the eye of the public; the trial before Pilate was held openly in a public forum.

15:1 *very early*. The court began at daybreak, making it necessary that the Sanhedrin meet in an all-night session. They were anxious to get a quick conviction before the people found out what they had done. ***decision.*** Legally, the Sanhedrin had no authority to order the death of Jesus (see Jn 18:31). The real reason they defer to the Roman legal system (as Mark makes clear) is their fear of the people (11:32; 12:12; 14:1-2). However, the difficulty they faced is that under Roman law, blasphemy was not a capital offense. Consequently, they needed to present the case to Pilate so as to ensure Jesus' death. Their decision was that when they brought Jesus to Pilate, they would charge him with high treason. ***led him away.*** They probably took him to the palace of Herod, located northwest of the temple, where Pilate stayed when he came to Jerusalem from his home in Caesarea. Pilate was probably in town for the feast. ***Pilate.*** Pontius Pilate was the fifth procurator of Judea. He served from A.D. 26-36. Historians of the time called him an "inflexible, merciless and obstinate" man who disliked the Jews and their customs.

15:2-5 Mark describes Jesus' interrogation by Pilate. The Roman trial consisted of the accusation, followed by an examination of the defendant by the magistrate. Once a ruling had been made, it was carried out immediately.

15:2 *king of the Jews*. This is how the Sanhedrin translated the Jewish title "Messiah" so that Pilate would understand it. Put this way, it made Jesus seem guilty of treason (he would appear to be disputing the kingship of Caesar). There is great irony in this title. Jesus has consistently refused to be the military Messiah pictured in popular culture, and yet now he will be condemned as a guerrilla! This title is used six times in chapter 15, and explains what it means for him to be the Son of God (which is the crucial insight in this section—see 15:39). ***Yes, it is as you say.*** As he accepts the title "the Christ, the Son of the Blessed One" from the Jewish high priest (14:61-62), he also accepts the title "king of the Jews" from the Roman procurator. In both cases, his questioners misunderstood the nature of the title they

attribute to Jesus. And in both cases, this misunderstanding led to Jesus' condemnation.

15:7 *Barabbas*. Barabbas was a genuine resistance leader, guilty of murder. According to the Greek text of Matthew 27:17, his full name was "Jesus son of Abbas" which provided another irony. The wrong "Jesus" was killed as an insurrectionist!

15:8 *the crowd*. It seems ironic that the crowd, who at the beginning of the week hailed Jesus as "he who comes in the name of the Lord" (11:9), could at the end of the week call for his crucifixion. In fact, it was very unlikely that this was the same crowd. There were over two million people in Jerusalem during the Passover. Jesus was arrested secretly, late at night. Now it is early the next morning. His supporters had little time to hear of his abduction, much less to arrive at the palace for his trial. A different group had gathered that morning. Possibly they were supporters of Barabbas (a hero to many), who wanted him released by means of the Passover amnesty (see v.6).

15:9-11 Pilate seems satisfied that Jesus is not a true insurrectionist. His desire to release Jesus probably had little to do with justice, and arose more out of a desire to do something that would annoy the Sanhedrin (with whom he had many run-ins).

15:12-14 Pilate seems surprised that the crowd rejects his offer to release Jesus.

15:15 *released Barabbas*. The death of Jesus (who is innocent) in the place of Barabbas (who is guilty) is a visual statement of the meaning of substitutionary atonement. It explains what Jesus meant in 10:45 when he said that he came to "give his life as a ransom for many." ***flogged.*** This was a terrible punishment. Soldiers would lash a naked and bound prisoner with a leather throng into which pieces of bone and lead had been woven. The flesh would be cut to shreds. ***crucified.*** Crucifixion was the most feared of all punishments in the first-century world. It was cruel in the extreme and totally degrading.

15:16-20 The soldiers mock Jesus as the Sanhedrin had done before them (see 14:65). Whereas the Sanhedrin mocked the idea that he was the Messiah, the soldiers mock the idea that he is king.

15:16 *soldiers*. Probably the troops that had accompanied Pilate on his trip from Caesarea.

[Notes continued on page 91]

Mark 15:1-41, continued

Questions

The Crucifixion

²¹A certain man from Cyrene, Simon, the father of Alexander and Rufus, was passing by on his way in from the country, and they forced him to carry the cross. ²²They brought Jesus to the place called Golgotha (which means The Place of the Skull). ²³Then they offered him wine mixed with myrrh, but he did not take it. ²⁴And they crucified him. Dividing up his clothes, they cast lots to see what each would get.

²⁵It was the third hour when they crucified him. ²⁶The written notice of the charge against him read: THE KING OF THE JEWS. ²⁷They crucified two robbers with him, one on his right and one on his left. ᵛ ²⁹Those who passed by hurled insults at him, shaking their heads and saying, "So! You who are going to destroy the temple and build it in three days, ³⁰come down from the cross and save yourself!"

³¹In the same way the chief priests and the teachers of the law mocked him among themselves. "He saved others," they said, "but he can't save himself! ³²Let this Christ, ʷthis King of Israel, come down now from the cross, that we may see and believe." Those crucified with him also heaped insults on him.

The Death of Jesus

³³At the sixth hour darkness came over the whole land until the ninth hour. ³⁴And at the ninth hour Jesus cried out in a loud voice, *"Eloi, Eloi, lama sabachthani?"*—which means, "My God, my God, why have you forsaken me?"ˣ

³⁵When some of those standing near heard this, they said, "Listen, he's calling Elijah."

³⁶One man ran, filled a sponge with wine vinegar, put it on a stick, and offered it to Jesus to drink. "Now leave him alone. Let's see if Elijah comes to take him down," he said.

³⁷With a loud cry, Jesus breathed his last.

³⁸The curtain of the temple was torn in two from top to bottom. ³⁹And when the centurion, who stood there in front of Jesus, heard his cry andʸ saw how he died, he said, "Surely this man was the Sonᶻ of God!"

⁴⁰Some women were watching from a distance. Among them were Mary Magdalene, Mary the mother of James the younger and of Joses, and Salome. ⁴¹In Galilee these women had followed him and cared for his needs. Many other women who had come up with him to Jerusalem were also there.

13. As an expert in such matters, why is the centurion's confirmation of Jesus' death (v.39) important? How does that confession complete the Gospel Mark set out to write (see 1:1; 8:29)?

REFLECT: 1. Why did Jesus go through this trial and torture when he easily could have used his great powers and escaped? How does this make you feel? What does it make you want to do? **2.** What do you think you would have done in Pilate's place? In Barabbas' place? In the soldiers' place? **3.** How could a loving God abandon his obedient Son—and for *my* sins? Read Isaiah 53:12. How would you paraphrase it to explain what Jesus' death was all about? **4.** What "curtain" do you feel still separates you from God? How does Jesus' death relate to that? **5.** What is the riskiest thing you have ever done because of your faith in Jesus? Why did you do it? What were the results?

ᵛ27 Some manuscripts *left,* ²⁸ *and the scripture was fulfilled which says, "He was counted with the lawless ones"* (Isaiah 53:12) ʷ32 Or *Messiah* ˣ34 Psalm 22:1 ʸ39 Some manuscripts do not have *heard his cry and.* ᶻ39 Or *a son*

Notes, continued

15:21-39 This is the culmination of Mark's Gospel. It is the death of Jesus that will unlock all the mysteries and open the way into the kingdom of God. This section is rich with allusion to OT prophecy.

15:21 Simon. Possibly a Jew, from a Greek city on the north shore of Africa, who had come to Jerusalem for the Passover feast. **Rufus**. Romans 16:13 mentions a Rufus. Mark wrote his Gospel for the church at Rome, and if this is the same Rufus, he can verify this detail about their father. **carry the cross**. The prisoner carried the heavy cross-beam through the winding streets as an "example" to others.

15:22 Golgotha. in Aramaic, "a skull." This was probably a round, bare hillock outside Jerusalem.

15:23 wine mixed with myrrh. It was a Jewish custom to offer this pain-deadening narcotic to prisoners about to be crucified (see Ps 69:21).

15:24 they crucified him. Mark has looked to this event throughtout his Gospel. When it happens, he records it in the simplest, starkest way. Josephus, the Jewish historian, calls it "the most wretched of all ways of dying." The person to be crucified was first stripped. Then his hands were tied or nailed to the cross-beam. This was lifted to the upright stake, and then the feet were nailed in place. **dividing up his clothes**. The clothes of the condemned person belonged to the four soldiers who carried out the crucifixion (see Jn 19:23-24; Ps 22:18).

15:26 the written notice. The crime for which the person was being crucified was specified on a whitened board fastened above the criminal.

15:27 robbers. This was a term sometimes used for Zealots, the band of nationalists who were committed to the violent overthrow of Rome. While "robbery" *per se* was not a capital crime, insurrection was. Perhaps they were involved with Barabbas in the incident mentioned in 15:7. In any case, the reference to being crucified alongside criminals is probably an allusion to Isaiah 53:12.

15:29-32 These insults and mocking statements fulfill Psalm 22:6-8.

15:31 He saved others . . . but he can't save himself. This is just the point! Because he is saving others, his own life is forfeit. Once again Mark uses irony. Something true is said about Jesus by a person who does not understand the accuracy of the statement (see 14:61-62; 15:2).

15:33 at the sixth hour. At noon. **darkness**. A supernatural event, showing the cosmic significance of this death. See Amos 8:9. There is darkness from the time Jesus is hung on the cross until he dies.

15:34 It is uncertain what Jesus' cry meant. Certainly he experienced the consequences of being cut off from God because of the sins of many (see Ps 22:1).

15:35 Elijah. Another irony. Elijah already came in the person of John the Baptist (see note on 9:4).

15:36 Wine vinegar was considered a refreshing drink (see Ru 2:14). A soldier soaked a sponge in wine vinegar and water and offered it to Jesus.

15:37 a loud cry. This is unusual. Generally the victim is exhausted and unconscious at the point of death. It is almost as if Jesus voluntarily gives up his life. Perhaps what Mark mentions here is the last word in the phrase "It is finished" (see Jn 19:30).

15:38 curtain of the temple. There were two curtains in the temple. An outer curtain separated the sanctuary from the courtyard. The inner curtain covered the Holy of Holies where only the high priest was admitted. It is not clear which curtain was torn. However, the point is clear: that which stood between the people and God was abolished by Jesus' death.

15:39 This confession concludes the second half of Mark's Gospel. In 1:1, Mark stated that what he was writing was the good news about Jesus the Messiah, the Son of God. The first half of the Gospel ends with the confession of Peter (a Jew) that Jesus is the Messiah (8:29); the second half ends with the confession of the centurion (a Gentile) that Jesus is the Son of God. **centurion**. The supervising officer, a pagan soldier who may not have been aware of the significance of what he observed.

15:40 some women. Mark names three eyewitnesses of the crucifixion. Mary Magdalene was from the village of Magdale on the west coast of Galilee (see Lk 8:2). The other Mary had well-known sons in the early church. Salome was the wife of Zebedee and the mother of James and John (Mt 27:56). In contrast, all the disciples have fled.

UNIT 26   The Burial of Jesus/The Resurrection

Mark 15:42-16:20

The Burial of Jesus

⁴²It was Preparation Day (that is, the day before the Sabbath). So as evening approached, ⁴³Joseph of Arimathea, a prominent member of the Council, who was himself waiting for the kingdom of God, went boldly to Pilate and asked for Jesus' body. ⁴⁴Pilate was surprised to hear that he was already dead. Summoning the centurion, he asked him if Jesus had already died. ⁴⁵When he learned from the centurion that it was so, he gave the body to Joseph. ⁴⁶So Joseph bought some linen cloth, took down the body, wrapped it in the linen, and placed it in a tomb cut out of rock. Then he rolled a stone against the entrance of the tomb. ⁴⁷Mary Magdalene and Mary the mother of Joses saw where he was laid.

The Resurrection

16 When the Sabbath was over, Mary Magdalene, Mary the mother of James, and Salome bought spices so that they might go to anoint Jesus' body. ²Very early on the first day of the week, just after sunrise, they were on their way to the tomb ³and they asked each other, "Who will roll the stone away from the entrance of the tomb?"

⁴But when they looked up, they saw that the stone, which was very large, had been rolled away. ⁵As they entered the tomb, they saw a young man dressed in a white robe sitting on the right side, and they were alarmed.

⁶"Don't be alarmed," he said. "You are looking for Jesus the Nazarene, who was crucified. He has risen! He is not here. See the place where they laid him. ⁷But go, tell his disciples and Peter, 'He is going ahead of you into Galilee. There you will see him, just as he told you.' "

⁸Trembling and bewildered, the women went out and fled from the tomb. They said nothing to anyone, because they were afraid.

Questions

OPEN: 1. How do you feel deep down when you attend funerals and burials? **2.** What is the most unbelievable event you've ever witnessed?

DIG: 1. What is significant about the eyewitnesses of his burial (vv.40-41,47; see Mt 28:11-15)? **2.** Why do you think the women go to the tomb at the time they do? What does this say about them? Where have their thoughts been since Friday? **3.** What potential problem looms ahead? What do they find instead? What do they fear? Seeing the empty tomb and the man sitting beside it, what thoughts are racing through their heads? **4.** Do you think they believed the man? How do their actions support your answer? **5.** Why do you think the angel asked the women to speak to the disciples, and to Peter specifically? What does this tell you about Jesus' plans for Peter?

REFLECT: 1. Would you have had trouble believing the angel's words? Why or why not? **2.** Who did Jesus send to you to tell you he had risen? Did you have trouble believing that person? How were you finally convinced of Jesus' resurrection? **3.** To whom is Jesus sending you with this message? How will you accomplish this mission? **4.** Where is your spiritual life focused these days: On Good Friday? Easter Sunday? Or in between?

[Scripture and questions continued on page 94]

Notes

15:42 *Preparation Day*. Jesus died on Friday at 3:00 p.m. The Sabbath began at 6:00 p.m., after which no work could be done. Great haste was required.

15:43 *Joseph of Arimathea*. Little is known of him, except that he was from a wealthy and prominent family and was a member of the Sanhedrin. (Possibly he was the source of information about Jesus' trial before the Sanhedrin.) To ask for the body was to admit allegiance to the now discredited Jesus and was, therefore, potentially dangerous. Often the Romans just left the bodies hanging on the cross to be eaten by vultures, though they did grant requests by the family to be allowed to bury the person. However, the Romans almost never allowed those convicted of treason to be buried. The fact that they do so now probably means Pilate knew Jesus was innocent (see the note on 15:9-11).

15:44 *Pilate was surprised*. It often took two or three days for a person to die.

15:45 The centurion confirms that Jesus had died in six hours. As a supervisor of crucifixion, he had expert insight into such matters. Therefore, when Jesus rose several days later, it was resurrection, not resuscitation.

15:46 The body was washed, quickly wrapped, and then placed in a tomb (probably a natural cave or an abandoned quarry). The tomb was then sealed against robbers or animals by means of a large stone. This was all done hurriedly, due to the approach of the Sabbath. Joseph, being wealthy, probably had servants to assist him in this task. **linen**. The young man in 14:51 left behind a linen cloth, anticipating how Jesus would be clothed after his death.

15:47 Two of the three women at the crucifixion saw clearly where Jesus was entombed, so when they returned in two days, they knew where to go.

16:1-8 Mark tells the story of the resurrection in brief, crisp terms. This account does not describe the resurrection as such, only the discovery of the empty tomb by the women and the explanation given by the "young man." In fact, none of the Gospels try to describe the resurrection; only the fact that it had taken place.

16:1 *when the Sabbath was over*. After 6:00 p.m. on Saturday when the shops were open again. **spices**. Aromatic oils to anoint the body, not so much to preserve it as to honor it (much like people today would put flowers on a grave). See Mark 14:3-9. Clearly they did not expect Jesus to have risen from the dead, since the perfumes they bought would have been quite expensive.

16:2 *very early on the first day*. Early Sunday morning.

16:3 *the stone*. It would have been fairly easy to roll the huge, disc-shaped stone down the groove cut for it so that it covered the opening; but once in place, it would have been difficult to push it back up the incline. **tomb**. Typically, such tombs had a large antechamber, with a small two-foot high doorway at the back which led into the six- or seven-foot burial chamber proper. This was the tomb of a wealthy family. See Isaiah 53:9, which says the suffering servant would be buried with the rich.

16:4 The stone was rolled away, not so that the resurrected Jesus could leave the tomb, but so that his disciples could see that it was empty (see Jn 20:8).

16:5 *a young man*. An angel (see Mt 28:2-3). The particular word Mark uses here was used in other contexts to refer to an "angel." Angels were often used as messengers of God's revelation. His words explain why the the tomb is empty by revealing to the women the resurrection of Jesus. **a white robe**. An indication of his heavenly nature. Jesus was clothed in dazzling white during his transfiguration (9:3). **alarmed**. A rare Greek word used in the NT only by Mark (see also 9:15; 14:33), indicating great astonishment in the face of the supernatural.

16:6 *He has risen!* In the same way that Mark reports the crucifixion of Jesus in simple, stark terms (15:24), so too he describes his resurrection in a plain, unadorned way. The phrase is, lit., "he has been raised," showing that God is the one who accomplished this great act. His resurrection demonstrates that the cry of the centurion was accurate: "Surely this man was the Son of God!" (see Ro 1:4).

[Notes continued on page 95]

Mark 15:42-16:20, continued

Questions

[The most reliable early manuscripts and other ancient witnesses do not have Mark 16:9-20.]

⁹When Jesus rose early on the first day of the week, he appeared first to Mary Magdalene, out of whom he had driven seven demons. ¹⁰She went and told those who had been with him and who were mourning and weeping. ¹¹When they heard that Jesus was alive and that she had seen him, they did not believe it.

¹²Afterward Jesus appeared in a different form to two of them while they were walking in the country. ¹³These returned and reported it to the rest; but they did not believe them either.

¹⁴Later Jesus appeared to the Eleven as they were eating; he rebuked them for their lack of faith and their stubborn refusal to believe those who had seen him after he had risen.

¹⁵He said to them, "Go into all the world and preach the good news to all creation. ¹⁶Whoever believes and is baptized will be saved, but whoever does not believe will be condemned. ¹⁷And these signs will accompany those who believe: In my name they will drive out demons; they will speak in new tongues; ¹⁸they will pick up snakes with their hands; and when they drink deadly poison, it will not hurt them at all; they will place their hands on sick people, and they will get well."

¹⁹After the Lord Jesus had spoken to them, he was taken up into heaven and he sat at the right hand of God. ²⁰Then the disciples went out and preached everywhere, and the Lord worked with them and confirmed his word by the signs that accompanied it.

REFLECT: 1. Would you have had trouble believing the angel's words? Why or why not? 2. Who did Jesus send to you to tell you he had risen? Did you have trouble believing that person? How were you finally convinced of Jesus' resurrection? 3. To whom is Jesus sending you with this message? How will you accomplish this mission? 4. Where is your spiritual life focused these days: On Good Friday? Easter Sunday? Or in between?

Notes, continued

16:7 *go, tell*. Under Jewish law, women were not considered reliable witnesses. That they were the first to know of the resurrection was an embarrassment to the early church (see Lk 24:11, 22-24), hence guaranteeing the historicity of this detail. ***his disciples and Peter***. They may have abandoned Jesus, but he has not abandoned them! A special word is given to Peter who, after his abysmal failure, might be tempted to count himself out of further discipleship. Forgiveness is offered. Paul mentions that one of the Lord's post-resurrection appearances was to Peter alone (1Co 15:5; Lk 24:34). ***into Galilee***. Jesus said he would meet them again in Galilee (14:28). The ministry of Jesus and the Twelve began in Galilee, and now they are directed back there to meet the risen Lord, thus bringing Mark's account full circle. See Matthew 28:16-20 for the account of that meeting.

16:8 *they said nothing*. Eventually, of course, the women did report what happened (see Mt 28:8; Lk 24:10). ***they were afraid***. This was the same sort of fear that the disciples felt on the Sea of Galilee when they discovered that Jesus had power over the elements themselves (4:41). This is how human beings respond in the face of the supernatural. Thus the Gospel of Mark ends on this note of astonishment and fear which was so characteristic of how he described people's reaction to a miracle or supernatural event (2:12; 4:41; 5:15, 33, 42; 9:6). There is also the hint of mystery and secret, again characteristic of Mark. The ending is abrupt, but fully in keeping with Mark's style of writing.

16:9-20 Scholars generally agree that these verses were composed at a later date by another author. They do not appear in the best ancient manuscripts, and they have a vocabulary and structure quite different from the rest of Mark. (This is seen most readily in the Greek.) This particular ending seems to have been a summation of resurrection stories found in the other Gospels, along with a list of miraculous signs that occurred in the early church. As such, this ending is an early and interesting part of the Christian tradition, but it is not the words of St. Mark. This ending (16:9-20) is but one of several that have appeared in ancient manuscripts of Mark. This is testimony to the fact that early scribes found Mark 16:8 too abrupt. One of the other endings reads as follows: "But they reported briefly to Peter and those with him all they had been told. And after this Jesus himself sent out by means of them, from east to west, the sacred and imperishable proclamation of eternal salvation." Some scholars feel that the original ending of Mark was lost, though there is no concrete evidence that this is the case.

16:17-18 Although no mention is made of such signs in the other Gospels, such things did happen in the early church (see Ac 2:43; 4:30; 5:12; Heb 2:4). ***they will speak in new tongues***. See Acts 2:4; 1 Corinthians 14:18. ***they will pick up snakes***. See Acts 28:1-6. ***drink deadly poison.*** There is no mention of this elsewhere in the NT. ***they will place their hands on sick people and they will get well***. See Acts 3:1-10; James 5:14-15.

ACKNOWLEDGMENTS

In writing these notes I have made use of the standard research tools in the field of New Testament study. These include *A Greek-English Lexicon of the New Testament* (Bauer, Arndt & Gingrich), *The Interpreter's Dictionary of the Bible, The Macmillian Bible Atlas* (Aharoni & Ave-Yonah), *The NIV Complete Concordance, Synopsis of the Four Gospels* (Kurt Aland) and other standard reference materials. In addtion, use has been made of various commentaries. While it is not possible as one would desire, given the scope and aim of this book, to acknowledge in detail the input of each author, the source of direct quotes and special insights is given.

The key commentary used in analyzing Mark is *Commentary on the Gospel of Mark* (The New International Commentary on the New Testament), William L. Lane, Grand Rapids, MI: Eerdmans Publishing Co., 1974. Other commentaries that were of special value include: William Barclay, *The Gospel of Mark* (The Daily Study Bible Series), Philadelphia: The Westminster Press, 1975 (Revised Edition) and Larry W. Hurtado, *Mark* (A Good News Commentary), San Francisco: Harper & Row, 1983.

Reference was also made to the following commentaries: Hugh Anderson, *The Gospel of Mark* (New Century Bible), Greenwood, S.C.: The Attic Press, Inc., 1976; Robert G. Bratcher and Eugene A. Nida, *A Translator's Handbook on the Gospel of Mark* (Help for Translators, Vol. II) United Bible Societies, 1961; R.A. Cole, *The Gospel According to St Mark* (Tyndale New Testament Commentaries), London: The Tyndale Press, 1961; Ezra P. Gould, *A Critical and Exegetical Commentary on the Gospel According to St. Mark* (The International Critical Commentary), Edinburgh: T. & T. Clark, 1969; William Hendriksen, *Exposition of the Gospel According to Mark* (New Testament Commentary) Grand Rapids, MI: Baker Book House, 1975; C.S. Mann, *Mark* (The Anchor Bible), Garden City, NY: Doubleday & Co., 1986; C.F.D. Moule, *The Gospel According to Mark* (The Cambridge Bible Commentary on the New English Bible), Cambridge: Cambridge University Press, 1965; D.E. Nineham, *The Gospel of Saint Mark* (The Pelican New Testament Commentaries) Harmondsworth, Middlesex, England: Penguin Books, Ltd., 1963 and Vincent Taylor, *The Gospel According to Mark*, NY: St. Martin's Press, 1966.

Reference was also made to: Craig Blomberg, *The Historical Reliability of the Gospels*, Downers Grove, IL: InterVarsity Press, 1987; F. Ross Kinsler, *Inductive Study of the Book of Mark*, South Pasadena: William Carey Library, 1972; R.H. Lightfoot, *The Gospel Message of St. Mark*, Oxford: Oxford University Press 1950; Ralph Martin, *Mark: Evangelist and Theologian*, Grand Rapids, MI: Zondervan Publishing House, 1973; and William Telfor (ed.) *The Interpretation of Mark*, Philadelphia: Fortress Press, 1985.

Richard Peace